PERCEPTUAL-MOTOR
— Theory and Practice

HAROLD A. LERCH
JOHN E. BECKER
BONNIE M. WARD
University of Florida
Gainsville, Florida

JUDITH A. NELSON
Elementary Physical
Education Specialist
Gainsville, Florida

Peek Publications • Box 11065 • Palo Alto, California 94306

Copyright 1974

Peek Publications

Fourth Printing 1980

ISBN 0-917962-36-2

#2107877

Manufactured in the United States of America

Dedication

We would like to dedicate this book to our parents, our spouses, and our children without whose love and inspiration this book could not have been written.

Preface

This book has been written for the teacher and college student who desires to become acquainted with the perceptual-motor development concept from both a beginning theoretical and practical viewpoint. This topic is certainly one of the most important areas of consideration in education today. This is especially true in light of the increasing focus of attention given to early childhood education programs throughout the country. For it is here and in the primary grades that the words "perception" and "motor" assume special significance in relation to learning. This relationship must be continually studied and understood by all teachers if we are to enhance the child's ability to learn. We must ask ourselves how does movement behavior, which implies sensory stimulation, affect this learning process? Is learning an abstraction made more concrete through the senses? For the child does the word "rabbit" take on greater meaning when he is allowed to see, feed and maybe even touch a live one?

The first half of this book deals with these and other related questions. You will notice that the term "theory" is used in this book when referring to perceptual-motor learning. It should be understood that this topic is yet in its theoretical stages. Investigators and practitioners alike have developed specific theories which will be discussed in later pages. They are based upon research findings and empirical evidence which indicates that a strong relationship exists between motor development and learning. These theories however, are not universally accepted for reasons stated elsewhere in the book. We hope that from the information presented you will be able to draw some preliminary first hand conclusions concerning the worth of these theories rather than relying on hearsay alone.

The second major part of this book deals with an exciting variety of playground and classroom activities designed to improve and reinforce motor development and classroom skills. They emphasize that learning can be fun and profitable when students are encouraged to "do" what they are learning in unique and challenging ways. These activities are also presented with the knowledge that not all children learn alike or at the same rate of speed. Thus, you may pick and choose those activities which you believe will be of greatest benefit to your students. We also wish to present you with the challenge of deciding when to proceed from simple to more difficult activities for your children. This we leave to your better judgment and sensitivity. We do, however, offer one general suggestion; permit your children to experience success by starting them at a level at which they can comfortably achieve. Remember that at the heart of every learner lies a self-concept. As a further guide these activities have been sequentially ordered from simple to complex in nature, based upon our best judgment.

Our hope is that after reading the theories and program suggestions contained herein, you will have a workable understanding in the area of perceptual-motor learning. Such is our purpose for writing this book.

Harold A. Lerch
John E. Becker
Bonnie M. Ward
Judith A. Nelson

Contents

Part I--Developing an Understanding
  Of Perceptual-Motor Learning

Chapter One: Moving Toward Discovery   3

Chapter Two: How Do Children Learn?   11
  Piaget, Hebb, Delacato, Kephart,
  Getman, Cratty
  Critique.   33
  Bibliography   36

Chapter Three: The Effectiveness of Perceptual-
             Motor Function: Fact or Fiction?   37
  Educable Mentally Retarded.   37
  Normal Children.   40
  Underachieving Children   41
  Some Implications of Perceptual-Motor Research   42
  A Need for More Investigation.   47
  Bibliography   48

Part II--Screening for Perceptual-Motor Difficulties

Chapter One: A Basic Survey   55
  Large Muscle Screening Instrument   56
  Fine Muscle Screening Instrument   59

Chapter Two: Other Instruments.   61
  Tests and Assessment Tools   61

Part III--Designing an Action Program

Chapter One: A Team Approach   69
  Jimmy   71
    The Problem   71
    The Approach   71
    The Treatment.   72
    The Results   74
    Summary   75

Chapter Two: Developmental Activities 77
   Classroom Activities
      Pre-reading Skills 80
      Reading 81
      Pre-writing Skills 87
      Writing 88
      Mathematics 90
      Spelling 97
   Playground Activities
      Balance 99
      Coordination 109
      Coordination: Eye-Hand 110
      Coordination: Eye-Foot 118
      Coordination: Symmetrical 125
      Space and Direction . . . . , ... 132
      Body Image 135
      Rhythm 142

Appendix: Teaching Materials 147
   Books 147
   Films 149
   Filmstrips 150
   Records 152
   Teaching Aids 153
   Homemade Equipment 156

PART I
Developing an Understanding
of Perceptual-Motor Learning

CHAPTER ONE

Moving Toward Discovery

I hear and I forget
I see and I remember
I do and I understand
            Chinese Proverb

Johnny has a problem. Outwardly he looks like any other normal, healthy six year old boy. His eyes are bright and expressive, and he seems eager to learn. Yet beneath his carefree exterior there is a deeply troubled little boy. For you see, Johnny is not keeping pace with his classmates when it comes to learning in the classroom. Johnny's parents, both college educated and above average in intelligence, are at a loss to understand why their son is having this difficulty. Johnny's first grade teacher agrees with his parents and adds, "Johnny appears to be bright and intelligent but there seems to be some obstacle that he cannot overcome." By all the standards normally used to determine the learning ability of children this youngster should be an average achiever. For example, he scores well within the average range on I.Q. tests. Yet when it comes to his performance in the classroom, he consistently ranks below average.

Is Johnny an isolated case? Do other children suffer from similar "mysterious" learning problems? Well, let us look at some of Johnny's classmates and see. Mary hates to read. As each day goes by she becomes more frustrated because she cannot read. Billy claims his stomach hurts when it is time for the class's arithmetic lesson. Mike appears to know how to write and he has a lot of good ideas, but they are very hard for someone else to understand because Mike writes some of the letters of the alphabet backwards.

ㅏɑↃ (cat)

ɑnb (and)

3

Obviously, Johnny is not an isolated case at all. In fact, educational experts have estimated that as many as four out of every ten elementary school children in the United States today may have unexplained learning problems. The majority of these children are like Johnny and his friends in that their learning problems are not readily explainable. One can, therefore, begin to realize the crucial importance of understanding how children learn and of discovering how breakdowns in the learning process occur. Only through such an understanding is it possible to really help children with learning problems.

If certain estimates are correct four of these children could have
learning problems.

Let us take a closer look at Johnny. In the course of a normal school day he seems to be less active than most of his friends, especially on the playground. He usually stands out because he does not join in. When his friends are happily playing games, Johnny can usually be found standing on the sidelines just watching. But even when he does occasionally join in, his movements are awkward and clumsy. For some reason the ball eludes Johnny when he tries to kick it, yet it finds the tip of his nose quite well when he tries to catch it.

Is there a connection between Johnny's learning problems in the classroom and his poor motor performance on the playground? It seems as though his friends who are also having problems in the classroom also have movement problems while at play. Mary, our frustrated reader, continually loses her balance while trying to walk across a balance beam. Billy, who becomes upset just thinking about arithmetic, has unusual difficulty in attempting to tie his shoelaces. Mike, our backwards writer, does not know his right from his left.

Furthermore, he cannot identify some of his body parts nor can he coordinate their movements.

Cases such as these have caused people concerned with children's learning problems, to attempt to discover if there is a relationship between how children move and how they learn. The results of numerous scientific and empirical observations have convinced a growing number of these people that such a relationship does indeed exist. This concept is termed perceptual-motor theory because it appears that how an individual moves, how he perceives his surroundings, and his ability to learn are all somehow interrelated and interdependent.

But how? Well, first of all it is important to determine what is known about learning.[1] Actually, we do not really know a great deal about how children learn. Learning is called a "theoretical construct" because it is a process that cannot be seen and therefore must be inferred. Hence, the term perceptual-motor theory. Because it is not possible to look into the brain and see "learning" taking place

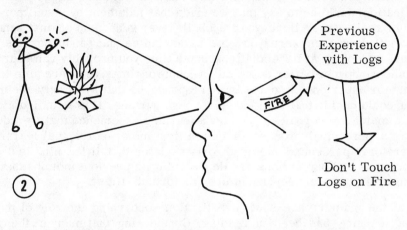

Sensory information comes into the brain and interacts with past information leading to behavior modification.

one can only make intelligent guesses as to how this process occurs. We do know, however, that in order for learning to take place there needs to be some type of sensory information transmitted to the brain.[2] Once this information reaches the brain it is interpreted and given meaning in light of previous information and called perception. Therefore, learning is dependent upon perceptions. If these perceptions are based upon previous motor experiences then we can see how learning is indeed motor based.

---

[1]Learning will herein be defined as those permanent changes in behavior brought about by experiences.

[2]It is necessary to make a distinction between sensation and perception. These two terms will be used throughout this book. Although these terms are very closely related, they are not synonymous. Sensation refers to information coming into the organism through the sensory organs. Perception, on the other hand, while being initiated by sensation involves interpretive processes in the brain and is, therefore, greatly influenced by learning.

Assume that Johnny and his friends do have learning problems that are motor based. How then did they come to have these motor problems? Experts in the area of child growth and development such as Jean Piaget tell us that children develop in stages. The earliest and most important stage is motor development. An infant in the first few weeks of his life, even before his eyes can focus properly, learns about his surroundings primarily through movement. He learns what a rattle is, for instance, by shaking it, by exploring it with his hands and mouth, and by bringing it close to him. These first crude motor explorations of the child's environment form the foundation of all future learnings.

You may say that is fine for a newborn baby but what has that to do with a school-age child? The school-age child, having a fairly well developed perceptual system, learns more about his environment through vision and hearing than through motor movements. That appears to be true, but upon what type of information does he base these perceptions? Let us take a piece of sandpaper for an example. When you look at sandpaper you know that it has a rough surface. Our first inclination would be to say that we made that judgment by visual perception. But is this really true? Have your eyeballs ever rubbed up against sandpaper? We hope not! How then were you able to determine that sandpaper has a rough surface just by looking at it? Actually, at some time you probably ran your fingers across some sandpaper. After doing this a couple of times you were able to translate this motor experience into a learned response, so that by simply seeing sandpaper you could decide that it is indeed a rough surface. This is called a perceptual-motor match. Now you can see how a learning experience that we would tend to label as a perceptual process is in reality a motor-perceptual learning process. Therefore, perceptual-motor theorists claim that if learning is dependent upon perceptions and perceptions are dependent upon previous motor experiences, then learning is ultimately dependent upon motor activities.

One of the primary areas of investigation concerning the role of the motor system in learning has been in reading. Considering that many of the children with learning problems have trouble learning to read and that reading forms the cornerstone of our entire educational system, we can appreciate why so much research has been concentrated in this area. Another reason for studying reading has been the very close connection between vision and previous motor experiences. Examples of this have already been discussed.

To help us further understand the relationship between the child's motor system and learning to read, let us take a closer look at Mary. Mary, like Johnny, is a child of "average" intelligence. Yet when she tries to read her progress is slow and painful. Mary's concerned parents took her to a vision specialist in hopes of finding a solution to her problem. Upon careful examination it was discovered that the muscles which control the movement of the eyes, were not functioning properly. Therefore, Mary did not have complete control over her eye movements. Obviously, it was very hard for her to follow the words in her book in an orderly way. In fact, when asked to read aloud, what emerged was a jumble of disconnected words and phrases. You see, her eyes were unable to move smoothly from left to right and to make matters worse, they jumped from line to line and skipped entire words as well. When asked to read line two, Mary read, "Run, Bob, go."

1. See <u>Bob</u> run.
2. <u>Run</u> Spot run.
3. Spot can <u>go</u>.

As you can see Mary's eyes jumped from line two, to line one, to line three. When her difficulty was finally discovered it became apparent that Mary's reading problem really stemmed from a visual perceptual problem based upon a motor deficiency.

Could it be that Johnny and his friends were somehow deprived of essential motor experiences during the crucial early period of their development?

Could there have been some type of breakdown in the developmental sequences of each of these children? If so, what could cause such a breakdown? Actually there are a number of different potential causes. One of the more obvious is neurological injury of some sort. Brain damaged children are often considered as being seriously impaired—mentally and/or physically. But one theory suggests that many so-called "normal" school children may have suffered very minimal brain damage at birth. This damage may be slight enough not to be easily detected, but still cause learning problems.

Another cause is cultural deprivation. It is easy to see the difference between a child who has been raised in a culturally enriched home and one not as fortunate. The culturally deprived child has not had nearly as many opportunities to touch and explore many varied objects. Consequently, his background of experiences is far below what it could be. Only recently has this factor been taken into consideration, however. We still tend to assume that all children entering our schools have had the same background of experiences to draw upon.

Two other causes of breakdowns in the developmental sequence of children are emotional stresses and physical impairments. In many instances, these factors are easily recognizable, but not always. Emotional trauma, for example, can have a devastating effect on development. Take the child who takes a bad fall at his first attempt to walk. Who can tell what effect this experience and the resultant hesitation to try again will have on the child's future development?

At this point a number of important questions need to be answered. First, "does the fact that the perceptual-motor concept, being essentially theoretical and controversial, mean that educational practitioners should take a 'wait and see' attitude and not attempt to apply these theories to their children until more research 'proof' is available?" No, it is our belief that research needs to be done on both the laboratory and action levels. This means that informed practitioners in the field can lend a great deal to our knowledge in this area through action research with their children. Secondly, "what is the target population of perceptual-motor concept programs in the schools?" It would appear as if the perceptual-motor concept would have its greatest application with children of "normal" intelligence who are underachieving. The earlier these children can be spotted the better, so preschool programs would not be too early. In the elementary school it would seem that kindergarten through grade three would offer the greatest opportunity to spot problems in the perceptual-motor area. After the third grade, indications are that learning problems become more specific. These programs can be initiated by classroom teachers or physical education specialists. Finally, "how can perceptual-motor theory be applied to the school setting?" In two ways, through screening tests and then through perceptual-motor developmental activities. The classroom teacher and/or the physical education specialist can easily administer a screening test which measures both the large muscle and fine motor abilities of their children who are experiencing learning difficulties. Part II of this book includes a basic large muscle and fine motor screening test. In addition several perceptual-motor tests are analyzed as to purpose, and how to order.

A word of caution is suggested at this point. Researchers who have conducted studies in this area have often found what appears to be a positive relationship between improvement in motor skills and improvement in learning areas such as reading. This research has been questioned, however, because certain extraneous factors have not been eliminated. For example, when improvement is noted, is it due to improved motor skills, attention span, concentration, attitude, self-image, or to the individual attention shown each child? Critics of the perceptual-motor theory contend that until these questions are answered satisfactorily there will be some doubt concerning the validity of the entire concept.

Despite their criticism, however, most critics admit that it is becoming increasingly more difficult to discount the role of the motor system in the development of learning, and that a great deal of research still needs to be done in this area. One very important factor which is often overlooked in the perceptual-motor controversy is the improvement of motor skills through a concentrated program of perceptual-motor activities. If there is a need to justify the inclusion of perceptual-motor activities in the daily program of children with learning, perceptual, and motor deficiencies such a justification can be made on the basis of demonstrated improvement in the motor realm. That is, when children who are involved in perceptual-motor programs improve both in motor ability and reading ability, we believe there is a cause and effect relationship between the two which may or may not be true. We can be sure, however, that these children who started off at low levels of motor skills did raise their motor skill level significantly. Therefore, if the development of good motor skills is important in the life of the child, programs of perceptual-motor activities for children with poor motor skills would appear to be essential and worthy of inclusion for these children, even if they did not lead to improvement in other areas.

It should be noted that not all children with learning problems have a perceptual and/or motor basis for the problem. Perceptual-motor theorists have occasionally become so excited about the potentialities of their research that they have suggested that perceptual-motor programs should be used to help all children with learning problems. It would seem reasonable to assume that many problems being experienced by children may be perceptual and motor based, but due to the complexities of the human organism and the limited knowledge we have of the learning process, it would not seem prudent to affix a "cure-all" label to the perceptual-motor concept.

Once the children with perceptual and/or motor deficiencies have been identified the next step is to organize the perceptual-motor team. No one person has the total expertise to deal with perceptual-motor deficiencies alone. If a child has problems in this area, he needs all the help he can get. This help should come from the classroom teacher, physical education specialist, reading specialist, the child's parents, a vision specialist, the school psychologist and other team members deemed appropriate to the particular situation.

After the perceptual-motor team has been organized each member will have a specific portion of the remedial program to administer. In the case of the physical education specialist and the classroom teacher it is imperative that the child continue to attend his regular physical education program rather than using the time to isolate him for remedial activities! In conjunction with his physical education program and based upon his specific areas of weakness, the child should be given an individual program of perceptual-motor developmental activities. For example, if the child has shown a marked weakness in balance, his individual program should be geared toward working on balancing activities.

Part III of this book is devoted to specific developmental activities to match the areas tested on the screening test. In each case if a child shows weakness in a particular area a number of activities are presented and suggestions are given for working with the child.

Later chapters will demonstrate how to practically apply perceptual-motor theory to specific school situations. Before doing this, however, the reader should understand the basic underlying theory of perceptual-motor development. Chapter Two of Part I is designed to give a clearly written synopsis of the foundational theories of the men who can be considered the developers of the perceptual-motor concept.

Chapter Three of Part I gives the reader a concise summarization of the research that has been conducted in the perceptual-motor domain within the past decade. Certainly, before attempting to conduct action research in the field it is essential to understand what previous research has indicated. The importance of knowing and understanding the nature of this research cannot be overstated.

CHAPTER TWO

How Do Children Learn?

"To learn to think, therefore, we should exercise our limbs, and our organs, which are the instruments of our intelligence . . ."
Rousseau's <u>Emile</u>

In the first chapter we met Johnny and some of his fellow students. It has been determined that these children have learning problems and that possibly there is a connection between their classroom difficulties and various motor problems they are experiencing. This perceptual-motor theory of learning is supported by several individuals from different fields such as psychology, optometry, and education. In this chapter we will examine the writings of some of the foremost perceptual-motor theorists in an attempt to understand why they believe that "all learning begins with movement." Until it is more clearly understood "how children learn" we will be handicapped in our efforts to help the Johnnys, Marys, Billys, and Mikes of this world."

Piaget

In trying to understand the process by which learning takes place, one logical starting point is to study children as they grow up. Through such a study one can try to find out how the helpless newborn goes about mastering the complex process of exploring and taking in information about his environment, and eventually develops the ability to deal with his environment symbolically (i.e., through the use of letters and numbers which make up our language). It is this ability of man, known as cognition, which separates him from the lower animals. One of the earliest investigators to study how children learn from the developmental point of view and to come to the conclusion that all higher learnings are based on early motor experiences was Jean Piaget. (9)

Piaget, the Swiss psychologist, has identified a number of developmental stages which he claims children pass through in the development of their cog-

11

nitive abilities. The first period of life Piaget labels the sensorimotor stage. This stage covers approximately the first two years of the child's life. During these years he changes from a self-centered infant who responds to his environment through primitive reflexes (such as sucking, etc.) to a child capable of rather complex sensorimotor[1] interactions with his environment. The period from age 2 to 11 is subdivided into two stages, the preoperational period and the period of concrete operations. The preoperational period (2-7) is characterized by the

Children first experience objects then verbalize concepts related to those objects.

child's initial attempts to deal with his world symbolically. The period of concrete operations (7-11) is the period in which the child begins to organize his understanding of his environment, and he develops the ability to knowingly adapt to changing situations. And, finally, there is the period of formal operations (11-15) in which the child develops the ability not only to deal effectively with concrete situations, but to deal with purely abstract situations as well.

Of these periods the sensorimotor stage is the most crucial, it is during this period that the foundations are laid for the higher learnings which will develop later. Therefore, let us look a bit closer at this period. Piaget terms this the sensorimotor period because it is during this period (before the child can speak) that the child lacks the ability to substitute abstractions such as words and thoughts for the concrete realities which they represent. This does not mean, however, that intelligence does not exist before language. On the contrary, it is generally accepted that intelligence does exist before language, and Piaget contends that it is a basically practical intelligence founded on sensory perceptions and movements. By "practical" he means that it is focused on getting results

---

[1]Sensorimotor here refers to the complex cycle whereby the child takes in information about his environment through his senses (touch, sight, smell, taste, etc.) and reacts to these sensations with a motor response.

which benefit the child. The child is, therefore, capable of solving movement problems, such as reaching distant objects, because he relates these problems to a movement vocabulary which he is developing. This vocabulary is made up of increasingly complex movement experiences which he has built up. Piaget has subdivided the sensorimotor stage into six substages. During Stage 1, or the first month of a child's life, he makes use of automatic reflexes such as sucking, swallowing, crying, and the like. The child is, of course, born with these reflexes and Piaget emphasizes that during this stage the child begins to modify his reflexive behavior in response to his environment. That is, the child soon begins to suck in response to stimulation around the area of the mouth. This represents the first stage of development in which the child starts the response rather than the response being solely reflexive.

Children learn to translate the visual image of an object into the
word representation of that object.

Stage 2, or the period from 1 to 4 months, is highlighted by the child developing the ability to coordinate the use of more than one sense at a time. He can, for example, reach out and touch an object brought into his field of vision, therefore, combining visual and tactile (touch) sensations in a coordinated manner. It is also during this period that the first simple habits are formed.

Stage 3, approximately from 4 to 5 months, is characterized by the child handling everything that comes near him. The child now has the ability to cause something to happen, or in other words he begins to assert control over his environment.

In Stages 4 and 5, a period from 8 to 18 months, the child begins to understand the difference between means and ends. He will, for example, attempt different methods to obtain an object out of his reach. He will then get to the point of searching for new means to reach a desired end, such as pulling a rug toward himself to obtain an object which he otherwise could not reach.

Finally, in Stage 6, which runs from 18 months to 2 years, the child begins to bridge the gap from this sensorimotor stage to the following period. He does this by inventing means to achieve desired ends, such as utilizing a stick to reach an object which is out of his reach.

Now consider Piaget's explanation of the development of perception. He is firmly convinced of the role of movement in the development of intelligence and states:

> "As regards the development of the cognitive functions in the child . . . the sensorimotor structures constitute the source of the later operations of thought. This means that intelligence proceeds from action as a whole . . ." (9, p. 28)

Piaget discounts the idea that mental life stems only from sensation and reason and does not involve action. To completely understand the error of this line of reasoning, he feels we must examine the role of the sensorimotor system in the development of perceptions. He points out that it is extremely difficult to follow the development of perception in the young infant because the baby cannot be subjected to precise laboratory experiments. There are, however, two visual perceptual abilities which can be studied in relation to sensorimotor functions during the first year. The first is constancy which may be subdivided into constancy of form and constancy of size.

Constancy of form refers to the perception of an object as it would appear from a frontal view, regardless of its present position. Constancy of size refers to the perception of the real size of an object when viewed from a distance, even though it appears to be shrinking. These constancies appear in the child about the middle of the first year.

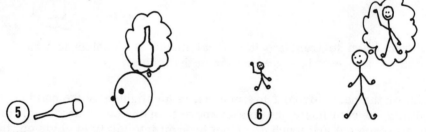

The child with properly developed constancy of form sees the bottle
from the bottom but percieves it in his mind in its upright position.
The child with properly developed constancy of size sees an object
at a distance, yet percieves it in his mind in its real size.

Piaget bases his belief that constancy of form is dependent upon motor activity on his observations of the relationship between constancy of form and the permanence of an object. He explains that a very young child discovers that objects are permanent through motor activities related to those objects. The child gradually comes to understand that when an object disappears, it does not cease to exist. Therefore, Piaget uses the example of a baby who is given a bottle with the bottom turned toward him who fails to recognize it as a bottle. Obviously, this child does not perceive a constant form of the bottle. However, later on, this same child readily turns the bottle around once he has learned to search for hidden objects (i.e., when he has established the permanence of objects), thus indicating that object permanence and constancy of form are related. Because of this, we can assume that an interaction takes place between perception and motor activity.

Piaget then points out that constancy of size appears after the child has developed the ability to coordinate the handling of objects with his vision. This helps explain why constancy of size cannot exist before this time. If visual and tactual sensations are not coordinated, the size of an object would remain constant to the touch but variable to the sight. Therefore, it is the sensorimotor development of the child which forms the basis for visual-tactual coordination essential to constancy of size perception.

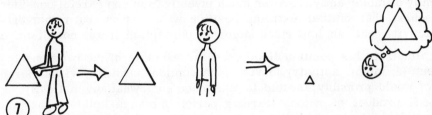

A child must coordinate what he sees with what he feels before he can perceive constancy of size.

Perceptual impressions of resistance, weight, and thrust are based on movement experiences with objects. Therefore, visual impressions of these phenomenon depend on prior motor experiences.

The second visual perceptual ability which can be determined in very young children is perceptual causality. If a child observes one object strike another and because of the impact the second object moves, the child has the impression that the first object caused the second to move. Depending on how the two striking objects react after impact, the observer has impressions of resistance, weight, thrust, etc. None of these impressions, of course, are visual in origin. This is, therefore, a case of tactual and kinesthetic impressions which have been translated into corresponding visual terms.

Piaget summarizes his beliefs on the development of perception by saying:

"Generally speaking, then we see that perceptual activities develop with age until they are able to obey the directives of the intelligence. But before the operations of thought are formed, it is the global action (motor activities) which performs the role of orientation." (9, p. 43)

Hebb

Another early theorist to support the notion that intellectual development is at least partially dependent upon motor development was D.O. Hebb. (7)

In his book, The Organization of Behavior, Hebb set about to clarify what he considered to be a misconception concerning the role of motor activity in perception. Psychologists had long before discarded the idea that perception was based solely on motor activity. This theory had been replaced, however, by what Hebb felt to be just as false a theory—that perception occurred completely independently of motor activity. After much investigation and careful consideration, Hebb decided that neither extreme position was correct, but rather that while motor activity was an important factor in perception it was not all-important.

To illustrate his position Hebb used the example of the relationship of eye movement (a motor activity) to visual perception. Ordinary visual perception, which we would probably assume to take place somewhat automatically, actually is the end product of a long learning period in man and other higher animals. Perceptual learning, according to Hebb, occurs gradually beginning with recognition of dominant colors, then proceeding to attention to the separate parts of a figure and ultimately culminating in the ability to recognize the whole figure. An infant must go through this complex learning sequence before he acquires the ability to recognize an object at a single glance.

In recognizing the form of a square, for example, the infant must first learn to identify the various parts of the figure over a period of time. Hebb feels that this identification depends upon visual scanning of the figure requiring a number of eye movements. The figure does not, at this stage of perceptual development, appear simply as a whole, but rather it appears to be several parts which are distinct from the whole. Once this first learning stage is mastered, Hebb points out that eye movements are no longer essential; but even for mature adults, eye movements definitely add to the clarity of perception.

Initially the young child scans an object with his eyes and recognizes its various parts. Once he has learned this, the child can recognize the object at a single glance.

Therefore, if we return to our example of the perception of a square, we can see that we did not always immediately recognize this figure as a square, but rather that this recognition is the result of a long, slow learning process which originally depended on many eye movements.

Closely associated with the above illustration is that of the relationship of eye movements to the formation of a visual image on the brain. Hebb contends that it would be difficult if not impossible to have an image of a given figure without making a number of eye movements. For example, in viewing a figure such as a triangle, circle, or square, a child would make several eye movements possibly jumping from point to point; but he would not simply fix the object in space. These eye movements, according to Hebb, not only improve the image but are essential to the development of vision.

The final step in this chain of logic is to answer the question concerning what role the motor area (cortex) of the brain plays in visual perception. Obviously, the motor cortex would not be involved at all unless perception was in some way closely related to motor activity. Since there is no evidence to support the possibility that the motor cortex of the brain actually receives visual sensation, it would, therefore, follow that it must somehow be involved with the changing of incoming sensations into visual perceptions. Hebb concludes his discussion of the importance of motor activity in visual perception by saying that:

> "Receptor adjustment (head-and-eye movement) is the most prominent feature of visual perception . . . except in long-practiced habits . . . eye movements in perception . . . contribute, constantly and essentially, to perceptual integration, even though they are not the whole origin of it." (7, p. 37)

Delacato

In 1959 a book was published which was destined to have a profound influence on the thinking of those individuals involved with children with learning problems —particularly those children with reading problems. This book, The Treatment and Prevention of Reading Problems, (4) by Carl H. Delacato, represented a departure from the traditional practice of seeking to correct reading problems by changing the system or method of teaching reading. Delacato points out that this approach has been tried time and again. Methods have been varied, and new methods have been invented to teach children to read; (such as sight recognition, phonetic, i.t.a., etc.) but invariably whatever method was used, some children would learn how to read and some would not. He, therefore, reasoned that some children would learn to read under any method, while certain other children would not learn under any method. This led him to look for the cause of reading problems not in the methods of teaching reading but rather within the children themselves.

Is there some factor or set of factors inherent within children which makes it either difficult or impossible for them to learn to read? If so, what are these factors and how may they be corrected? Delacato began a research project to attempt to answer these questions and others. He chose as subjects 45 boys[1] ranging in age from 8 to 10 who were experiencing reading problems. The results of this study indicated that there are at least a number of traits which seem to characterize the poor reader. All of these common traits were either physical or developmental. Delacato analyzed his results and decided that the primary area of concern was the neurological area. In other words, the problems which children with reading difficulties experience are in some way related to problems within their own central nervous system.

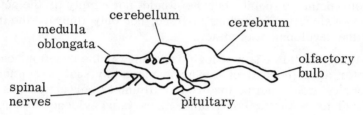

Typical animal brain (Alligator)

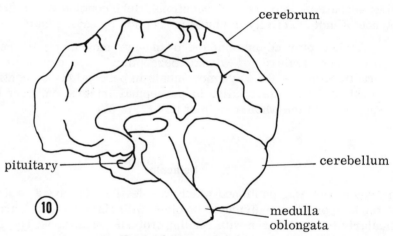

Typical human brain

In effect, Delacato's investigations revived the old theory that the neurological development of an individual follows the evolutionary development of the nervous system in man. That is, the nervous system of man represents the ultimate neurological development achieved in the animal kingdom. As the nervous system evolved through the centuries it has developed from a very simple to a very complex system. Most of man's central nervous system, such as the spinal cord, mid-brain, etc., resembled that of other animals. The primary difference, however, between man and the lower animals is the development of the cerebral cortex.

---

[1]He chose boys rather than girls because available research indicated that 4 boys have reading problems for every 1 girl experiencing the same problem.

It is this highly developed cerebral cortex of man that gives him the power of thought and reason which separates him from lower animals. The cerebral cortex, according to Delacato, allows man to develop cortical dominance through which one side of the body becomes dominant over the other (i.e., the cortex of the brain is divided into two parts [hemispheres]. The right side of the brain controls the left side of the body and vice versa. If the left side of the brain were dominant then the right side of the body would be also.) This is a highly desirable condition which when absent indicates that the individual has not gone through the proper neurological development pattern. He is, therefore, said to have neurological disorganization which results in reading and communication failures.

The importance of cerebral dominance lies at the heart of Delacato's theories concerning the treatment and prevention of reading problems in children. He points out that until about age six and one half, most children are ambidextrous (can use either hand equally well); at this time they usually develop a dominant eye, hand, and foot. This is also the time when reading is usually taught. This indicates that these functions are controlled by the dominant hemisphere of the brain and the dominant hemisphere should be the controlling hemisphere.   On the

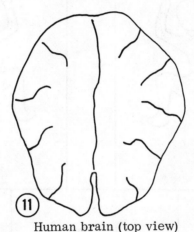

Human brain (top view)

The human brain is divided into two hemispheres. According to Delacato, if the left hemisphere is dominant, then the right side of the body should be dominant because the left side of the brain controls the right side of the body.

other hand, from birth the subdominant area of the brain controls the non-dominant functions such as tonality (the quality of tones such as music or the voice). Children exhibit tonal qualities at birth (making various sounds) and most tend to be left-handed, even though as they grow up most will become right-handed. Children, therefore, develop in the subdominant area first, but as they learn to talk and dominance appears on one side, we can assume that the dominant hemisphere is in control.

To support this position Delacato points out that children with brain damage in the dominant hemisphere who are unable to pronounce their own names have the ability to sing and in the course of a song may indeed pronounce their own names. Because of this tonality should be removed from the reading situation, and every effort should be made to definitely develop one dominant and one subdominant hemisphere.

Stuttering may also be used as support for this position. Delacato claims that stuttering is the result of lack of cerebral dominance. He uses the example that most stutterers do not stutter while singing and attributes this to the fact that during this period the subdominant area (which controls tonality) is actually in control.

Delacato also observed both good and poor readers during sleep and noticed a definite difference in the sleep pattern of both groups. When good readers sleep in a prone position (on their stomachs) their arms and legs are flexed on the side of the body which the head is facing, while the arms and legs on the opposite side are extended (see Ill. #12).

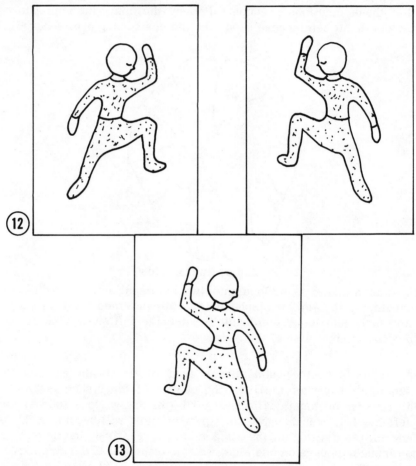

Delacato found that good readers sleep with their arm and leg flexed on the side of the body the head faces, even when the head changes from one side to the other.

When the head is turned in the opposite direction, a sequence of events occurs in which the arm and leg on the side of the body the head is facing flex, and the arm and leg on the opposite side extend (see Ill. #13).

Poor readers, it was found, do not sleep in this position, and if their heads are placed in this position the sequential reflex does not take place. This indicates a lack of neurological organization which prevents the sequential reflex action from taking place. This also explains why so many poor readers are classified as uncoordinated in movement activities such as running and walking. They simply do not have the neurological organization necessary to coordinate the movements in an efficient, meaningful pattern. Thus, without developing sequential patterns of movement, poor readers are uncoordinated at both the gross (large muscle) and fine (small muscle) motor levels.

Delacato also explains how slight brain damage in children may possibly cause reading disabilities. Obviously, those children with severe brain damage can be easily identified and would be expected to experience reading problems. But what about those children with very slight brain damage which is not easy to spot? For example, we know that anoxia (a lack of oxygen) for a period of three minutes can have a devastating effect on human brain cells. An infant deprived of oxygen for this period of time, either at birth or prior to birth, would surely be mentally handicapped because of the large number of brain cells destroyed due to the lack of oxygen. Delacato, therefore, reasoned that if three-minute oxygen loss caused severe brain damage, one-minute oxygen loss might also cause minor brain damage. This damage might not be great enough to be seen in obvious movement and mental handicaps, but may be enough to damage those highly sensitive brain cells responsible for the development of language.

The question then arises as to why four times as many boys experience reading problems as girls. Delacato explains this by citing evidence that boys heads tend to be larger at birth, thus lengthening the birth process and significantly increasing the period of time between dependence on the mother for oxygen and breathing for themselves. This would also help to explain why more firstborn children, as well as boys, tend to experience reading problems because deliveries of firstborn children are also slower.

Delacato investigated the role of vision in reading and came to some very interesting conclusions. He feels that visual dominance is just as important as hand and foot dominance in determining the ability of a child to read. Accordingly, hand, foot and eye dominance should all appear on the same side of the child's body if proper neurological organization is present. If the above conditions exist, the child should be able to read well.

Delacato points out that three qualities of vision should be evaluated to determine if proper neurological organization exists in the child. First, the dominant or the sighting eye should be determined. This is usually the eye used to look through a telescope (or a rolled up piece of paper). This eye serves a monocular (one-eyed) function, is established early in life, and stays the same throughout life. Secondly, the controlling eye should be determined. During binocular vision both eyes are used at the same time but one eye actually controls the perception while the other serves in an assisting roll. To determine your controlling eye hold your index finger out at arms length in front of you. Now pick out a distant object and with both eyes open "cover" the object with your index finger. Now close your left eye. If the object is still covered then your right eye is the controlling eye. If, however, the finger has "moved" the left eye is the controlling eye. This can be proven by now closing the right eye and opening the left. This "controlling eye" is not necessarily also the dominant eye. Contrary to the stability of the dominant eye, the controlling eye may be shifted due to changes in vision or actually be changed through training. Finally, the reading-visual function of each eye should be determined to find out which eye is more efficient. Testing by occlusion (covering of one eye) to see which eye reads material faster and with the fewest mistakes easily demonstrates the difference in efficiency of the two eyes. In each of the above mentioned cases, the dominant eye, the controlling eye, and the most efficient eye should be on the dominant side (i.e., the same side as the preferred hand and foot). If all three do not fall on the same side, crossed dominance and neurological disorganization is indicated and remedial measures (such as occlusion of the subdominant eye) are called for.

In his second book, The Diagnosis and Treatment of Speech and Reading Problems, (3) Delacato carefully traces the neurological development of the child. He describes the corresponding motor activity of each stage of development. He then compares the child's neurological development with animals that represent various levels of neurological development on the evolutionary scale (see Ill. #14).

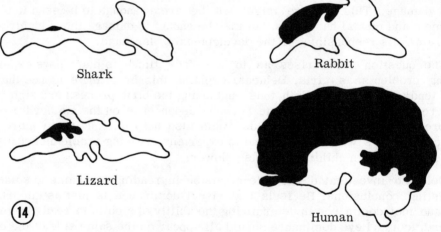

Shark

Rabbit

Lizard

Human

(14)

Various brains representing stages of neurological development within the animal kingdom. Dark areas indicate the relative proportion of brain area devoted to thinking.

For example, the behavior of the new born child is primarily reflexive in nature; that is, his actions are controlled by life-supporting reflexes such as breathing. These reflexes are under the control of the most primitive area of the human brain, the medulla oblongata. The child's motor actions at this time are fish-like in character and, indeed, the fish represents an animal which on the evolutionary scale develops no further than to this primitive neurological level.

At approximately four months of age, the child moves into the next neurological level. During this period the child begins to crawl. This method of locomotion is made with the body in contact with the floor and the body moved with homolateral movements of the arms and legs (i.e., with the arm and leg on one side of the body bent while the arm and leg on the opposite side are straight). This type of movement pattern is also typical of amphibians when in water and seems to be controlled by the pons.

⑮

4 month old child   Salamander

The pons represents the next step above the medulla in the neurological organization of the brain, and this is the most important part of the amphibian brain.

At approximately six months the child begins to creep. Creeping involves not only moving about on the hands and knees but doing so in a cross-pattern manner. Cross-pattern creeping means that as the child's left arm moves forward, his right leg moves forward at the same time. In his next movement his

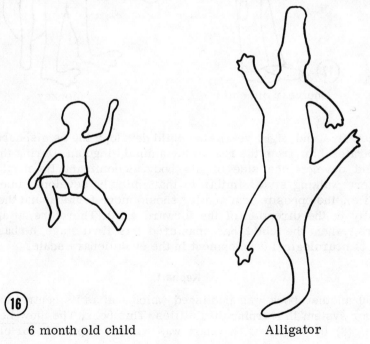

⑯

6 month old child   Alligator

right arm moves forward as his left leg moves forward. As he moves across the floor, he alternates his arm and leg movements in this manner, and he will also turn his head slightly in the direction of his forward hand. This activity is similar to the manner in which reptiles move across the ground and, according to Delacato, it is the mid-brain which controls this action in both children and reptiles. In reptiles the main feature of the brain is the mid-brain, and the child, therefore, has reached the neurological development level of the reptile or equal to the evolutionary stage of the mid-brain.

At around one year the child begins to pull himself up on furniture and begins a crude form of walking. This type of walking is characterized by the arms working independently of the legs, and Delacato points out that if the cross-patterning of the mid-brain stage is not mastered, the child will show signs of neurological disorganization and will have difficulty in mastering walking. This form of crude walking is typical of primates (mammals such as monkeys, which are considered to be on the nearest evolutionary level to man). Primates have brains in which the cortex is similar to that of a man. The cortex of primates does not, of course, develop the efficiency of the human cortex, so during this stage the child resembles a primate in displaying early cortical action.

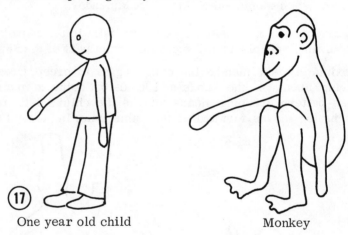

One year old child   Monkey

Between five and eight years, the child develops the hemispheric dominance which separates him from the rest of the animal kingdom. During this period the child should develop one side of his body as dominant. He should also have a cross-pattern walking style similar to that which he developed in cross-pattern creeping (i.e., the opposite arm and leg should move forward and the head should turn slightly in the direction of the forward arm). Therefore, at approximately eight years, when the child has mastered this final stage, he has reached the final level of neurological development in the evolutionary scale.

Kephart

In 1960 another book was published which had as its central theme the role of the motor system in learning disabilities. This book, The Slow Learner In The Classroom, (8) by Newell C. Kephart was written expressly for classroom and special teachers working with children with learning difficulties. The theme which this book, and a book interpreting Kephart's works written for the layman by D.H. Radler entitled Success Through Play (10), is based upon is that many children coming to school for the first time lack the "readiness" to learn. That is, we assume that children coming to school possess certain underlying abilities, such as being able to control their eye movements, which will allow them to achieve success in school. Dr. Kephart believes that many children are lacking these important perceptual and motor abilities, therefore, handicapping them in their efforts to learn. He also feels, however, that these readiness skills are as much learned as they are developed through maturation and that they can be taught in the school situation.

The complexity of the environment confronting a child, according to Kephart, makes any learning task difficult and demands that the child's behavior in response to his environment be flexible and coordinated. In tracing the growth of the young child, Kephart points out that children learn by doing. The child's very early responses to his environment are motor responses, and he is continually handling objects and moving his own body in relation to those objects so that he can understand his world motor-wise. Once he has established a "feel" for his environment, he begins to join together his motor experiences with sensory information coming to him through his eyes, ears, nose, mouth, and skin. Primarily it is his eyes which he uses as the extension of his arms to help him investigate objects which he cannot reach. The key point here is that the visual information which the child increasingly now uses is based upon motor information which he has gathered. He now begins to match incoming visual information with motor information as he handles and observes a given object at the same time. Over a period of time the "normal" child comes to develop a perceptual-motor "match" in which both systems give the child the same information. He actually learns to explore an object visually the same way he formerly explored it with his hands.

Kephart points out the importance of great amounts of experimentation involved in this process, and although to us this may seem rather aimless, it is for the most part very meaningful and should be started naturally by the child and not imposed on him by an adult. The problems which many children are experiencing in relating to an extremely complex society, however, are oftentimes caused by the fewer demands made upon children to explore on their own. The very fact that we as adults have tried to make growing up easier for our children by doing things for them or by substituting mechanical for manual toys has had the effect of not giving them many of the opportunities to explore, experiment, and touch which they must have to form a stable perceptual-motor system. Many children raised in this manner are coming into our schools unable to cope with the demands made upon them due to the lack of adequate perceptual-motor skills. For these children a great many opportunities to develop perceptual-motor skills through extensive exploration must be provided early in their school lives so that they will not become "slow learners."

To help explain the complexities of the underlying readiness skills necessary for a child to begin school, Kephart uses the example of a five-year-old child drawing a square. This seemingly simple task is actually only possible after many basic learning abilities are mastered. If we were to ask a child to sit at his desk and draw a square, one of the most basic large muscle abilities he would need to have would be the ability to sit up. Observation of a young infant attempting to sit will easily show us the great amount of time involved in learning to do this seemingly natural task. The child must, of course, learn to balance, vary tension among muscle groups, and develop the necessary strength to be able to sit up. The development of the large muscle skills necessary to maintain posture, therefore, underlie the child's ability to sit properly in a chair, so that he can draw the square.

Next the child must be able to coordinate the movements of his fingers, hand, wrist, and arm. This, again, seems to be a rather natural event, but as we know from observing children growing up, fine motor movements in the extremities develop only after mastery of central large muscle movements. That is, large movements of the arms come before movements in the wrist and hand which come before fine motor movements of the fingers. Thus, we can see that to be able to pick up a pencil and draw a square the child must have passed through a long period of learning in which he developed first his large muscle movements and finally his fine muscle movements. This would allow him to have enough control of his pencil to draw the square.

The child must also have enough muscular control to be able to call upon the proper muscles in the proper order to be able to accomplish the task of drawing the square. He must have the control to call upon just the right set of muscles without setting into action other sets of muscles. He must also be able to tell the difference between the movements of hand and fingers from total body movements as well as knowing one side of the body from the other.

This ability to tell one side of the body from the other is very important to what we call hand-eye coordination. We know that with the very young child movements are made at the same time on both sides of the body. Only after a great deal of experimentation does the child begin to distinguish movements which are made on the right side from those which are made on the left side. This basic understanding of right and left within the child's own body, known as laterality, is essential as a reference for the child from which he can draw the square.

The transfer of an internal awareness of right and left to an external awareness of the same thing, known as directionality, also must precede the ability to make a square. This "matching" of visual sensations against internal feelings (kinesthesis) of right and left obviously depends upon the child's ability to establish these relationships within himself. In other words, this visual understanding of our environment which we take so much for granted is actually based upon the kinesthetic foundation the child has established within himself. If these foundations have not been properly established, the objects which the child sees will not have dimensions such as right and left, up and down, etc., therefore, making such tasks as drawing a square and reading a book almost impossible to accomplish. Certainly, the common problem of word or letter reversals can be more easily understood if the child has no idea of direction. That is, the only difference between a "b" and "d" is one of direction, and the child lacking laterality and directionality sees no difference at all.

To make the square the child must also be able to make temporal (time)-spatial (space) changes easily. That is, he must be able to look at the square he is copying and see not separate lines and angles but an organized unity of lines and angles which in this relationship to one another form a square. When he draws the square, however, he cannot draw all of the lines at the same time but must draw them in a sequential pattern in time. To complete this task then we are asking the child to make this complex change from organization in space to organization in time.

Another task that the child must be able to handle before he can copy the square is to be able to separate the figure (square) from the ground (background). It is hard for us to imagine looking at a square or a printed page without seeing them as just that. Children, however, who have not developed proper form perception are apt to lose the square against its background and to confuse a printed word with elements in the background of the page. If the child has not developed this ability to distinguish parts of a figure from one another, then copying a figure such as a square or reading words on a printed page can be a hopeless task.

Taking Kephart's example of copying a square we can easily see that what we might have considered as a very basic task is, in itself, actually a complex skill requiring much previous learning.

Kephart continually stresses the fundamental role that the motor system plays in the development of higher forms of behavior. He states that:

> "It is logical to assume that all behavior is basically motor, that the prerequisites of any kind of behavior are muscular and motor responses. Behavior develops out of muscular activity, and so-called higher forms of behavior are dependent upon lower forms of behavior, thus making even these higher activities dependent upon the basic structure of the muscular activity upon which they are built." (8, p. 35)

It is easy to see that certain behavior depends upon movement when parts of the body can be observed moving in response to a given stimulus. But what about non-observable, internal behavior, however, such as thinking? Is the child, sitting apparently motionless in a chair just "thinking," actually using his motor system? According to Kephart he is. Experiments conducted while the subject's muscular responses to thought are measured by sensitive electrodes placed on the skin have indicated that both general overall muscular tension and specific muscular tension within certain muscle groups increase under these circumstances. Thus, what we might describe as "pure thought" processes actually involve muscular activity. It is therefore possible that the higher thought processes are no more efficient than the muscular responses upon which they are based.

One of the most basic of all movement patterns is that of posture. The importance of proper posture in copying a square has already been discussed. What other role does posture play in learning? It is through posture that we maintain a fixed orientation with our environment. If we are to have a set reference point from which to interact with the objects around us, it must be based on the force of gravity. We must establish a relationship with gravity through our own center of gravity and be aware of this relationship in all of our activities. Only through this stable relationship with gravity can we maintain a point of reference for interaction with our environment.

Closely related to posture as a point of reference for the body is laterality. Kephart explains that outside of our own body there is no information concerning direction. We develop information concerning right and left from within our own bodies. This information comes as the result of learning based on internal sensations about right and left. Every child must experiment with both sides of his body to determine their relationship to each other. Only through experimental movements of both sides of the body and comparing these movements and the differences between them with internal sensation can the child learn to tell the difference between right and left within his own body. The primary use of this information comes in relationship to balance. Maintaining balance is a problem which is constantly confronting children. Only with knowledge of and proper utilization of right and left can the child continually maintain his balance.

Once the child has developed laterality within his own body, he is ready to project this concept of right and left into the space around him. Again, this transfer of a concept takes place gradually after much experimentation. For example, the child will attempt to reach an object and in so doing he will notice that he must make a movement, perhaps to the right. By repeating this process a number of times, he will come to transfer the concept of right and left from within himself to objects in the space around him. At this point, of course, control of the eyes becomes a vitally important factor. Because the majority of information about our environment comes to us through our eyes, the development of directionality depends upon our visual system giving us the same directional information formerly obtained through kinesthesis.

Control of the eyes is also a very complex and exact motor task. The human eye is moved by six ocular muscles. These muscles have the task of moving the eye so that an image coming into the eye will fall on a small area at the back of the eyeball called the fovea. To accomplish this task the eye must be moved with great precision. Because of this, learning to control the movement of the eye is quite difficult. In time, however, the "normal" child will learn to match the movement of his eyes with the movement of his hands so that both systems will give him the same directionality information.

Yet another problem concerning directionality is that of midline. As the young infant begins to experiment with movement, he relates all movement to the vertical center of his body (midline). Using this as his point of reference, the child makes circular motions with his arms and legs at the same time. As his right arm moves toward the center of his body, the left arm moves toward the center of the body also. Moving his arms from outside in, therefore, involves going from left-to-right for his left arm and right-to-left for his right arm. A little later when the child begins to cross the midline of his body, we can easily see how confusion might set in, because to move the left hand left-to-right involves first an outside-in and then an inside-out pattern of movement. This new concept often causes children to hesitate and become confused as they cross the midline. Indeed, many older, slow-learning children show this same hesitancy and confusion.

The child learns to transfer information about his environment from motor to visual understanding through kinesthetic-visual matches. Therefore, the same transfer problem concerning crossing the midline can occur with the eyes that previously occurred with the hands. Thus, to avoid confusion the child must learn with great accuracy to locate the midline of his body and to always reverse the transfer of movement at the midline without disrupting the continuous movement. If this smooth transfer cannot be accomplished, the child will appear to be indecisive and lose control when his eyes cross the midline of his body.

To summarize the relationship of directionality to laterality, we can say that directionality is the transfer into the environment of the laterality developed within the child. Directionality is dependent upon laterality; and until the child has established solid concepts of laterality within himself, he will not have an accurate concept of right and left in space. To transfer laterality to directionality the child must make a match between visual information and kinesthetic information. To be able to do this the child must have exact control of his eyes and he must always know in what direction his eyes are pointed. Thus, the establishment of laterality and then the establishment of directionality is possible only through motor activity and the observations of motor activity.

If we accept Kephart's reasoning that the child establishes his own body as his point of reference in dealing with objects in his environment, it then follows that the child must have an accurate understanding of the dimensions of his body and the position of his body in space. Through various sensations (i.e., pressure, pain, etc.) we develop a picture of ourselves in our own minds. Through this "body image" we develop an understanding of the relationship of our body to other objects in space. Children who have not established a proper body image will continually over-estimate the amount of space necessary for them to perform certain movements. For example, such a child if asked to squeeze through a small space slightly larger than his own body will repeatedly bump into the boundaries of this space. He will also show great difficulty in moving various body parts independently of one another. If he begins to move his right arm, his left may move as well. He may also have difficulty transferring visual cues, such as when you point at a given body part, into muscular action or movement of the body part indicated. The child should be able to identify and control the various parts of his body independently if he has developed a proper body image.

In conclusion, Kephart states his belief that the input system, or perceptions and sensations, cannot be separated from the output system, or motor responses. He, therefore, encourages thinking and talking about these two systems as being part of the same closed cycle and stresses that:

> "We cannot think of perceptual activities and motor activities as two different items; we must think of the hyphenated term perceptual-motor." (8, p. 63)

Getman

Now that we have studied the claims of perceptual-motor theorists that motor activity forms the basis for visual perception, it would seem appropriate to get the reaction of a vision specialist to this point of view. One such specialist, G.N. Getman, an optometrist, has done research in this area and agrees with the findings of Kephart and others.

Getman points out that to the optometrist the eye is little more than a sensory organ which receives and reacts to light and changes light waves into electrical impulses which are sent to the brain. Somehow, these electrical impulses are combined in the brain with information coming in from other sensory systems. While optometrists need to know about the structure and operation of the eye, they have come to realize that to fully understand how the eye functions as part of a total visual system they must study more than just the eyes. For example, it is quite possible for two individuals to have eyes which when measured clinically appear to be exactly the same but which are functionally quite different. That is, one of these individuals may need his glasses constantly while the other may need his only for certain tasks, even though their prescriptions are exactly the same.

At this point it is essential that we understand the difference between sight and vision. Although we often use the two terms interchangeably, they are not synonymous. Getman defines sight and vision as:

> "Sight is the response of the eye to light, and its translation of this light into neural signals. Vision is the response of the total organism—the entire human being—to the information being collected throughout the total organism as a result of the light impact. Sight is the reception of light. Vision is the translation, utilization, and integration of the information, followed by the action of the totality in its use of this information. Whereas sight refers to the reaction of the eyes to light, vision refers to the entire complex of responses in all of the information systems as a result of the light impact. These primarily include the information systems of kinesthesis, touch, hearing, and several others. Sight can be isolated in the eyeball; vision cannot and must interchange with other systems."
> (6, p. 25)

Vision is, therefore, highly dependent upon the motor development of the individual.

Because of this relationship between motor development and vision, Getman feels that vision cannot develop fully without motor development. That is, the two systems are so dependent upon each other than one cannot operate efficiently without the other.

In attempting to discover the role of movement in vision, optometrists noticed that two individuals with eyes clinically equal yet functionally different also differed in movement skills. It was, therefore, concluded and clinically proven that knowledge of one's environment based on movement experiences within that environment led to greater visual development.

These clinical results encouraged Getman to study children to see if by improving their motor development there would be an equal improvement in their visual development. The results of this research indicated that, indeed, children's visual development could be aided in this manner.

Getman next decided to see how movement training compared with visual training instruments for eye patients needing clinical assistance. He placed his patients needing the most assistance into visually guided and evaluated movement programs and found that they quickly learned visual skills which they had not been able to master with the use of elaborate instruments. He found that patients acquired depth perception more readily by visually guiding themselves through space than by viewing three-dimensional pictures. Even one-eyed people can develop excellent depth perception through movement by following the same learning pattern that babies follow. Thus, optometrists have found that they can use movement to aid in the development of vision. They have also discovered a reverse effect that the development of the visual system has had on the general coordination of the patients observed. Many of these patients have become noticeably smoother and more coordinated in their muscular movements as a result of learning to use their visual systems as more reliable motor guidance systems.

One specific visual skill which optometrists and educators alike have linked to poor readers is tracking. Most poor readers have poor ocular tracking abilities (ocular tracking is simply eye movement following a moving target). The problem has been, however, that a great many good readers also have poor ocular tracking abilities. This has led optometrists to conclude that poor ocular tracking is not the cause of poor reading but that both poor ocular tracking and poor reading are signs of the child's inability to integrate his muscular movements effectively. Getman, therefore, points out the importance of not confusing ocular tracking with visual tracking (keep in mind the difference between sight and vision):

> "Visual tracking is the total ability to move the eyes across printed words in the proper direction and at the proper speed, scanning a word, phrase, or even a paragraph to glean as quickly, correctly, and effectively as possible the information they contain."
> (6, p. 26)

Although these two abilities involve the use of the eyes, they operate at different levels of performance.

Getman agrees with other perceptual-motor theorists about the importance of eye-hand coordination[1] to learning. He points out that although this ability has generally been taken for granted in both optometry and education, it actually forms the basis for the development of visual perception. That is, visual perception is based on the individual's ability to visually guide and evaluate his movements through space and his ability to explore his environment through touch and vision. Thus, visual perception develops through an integration of visual information with other sensory information (usually touch). The child must learn to interpret his environment at close range through touch and taste before

---

[1] It is interesting to note that optometrists refer to it as eye-hand coordination while physical educators refer to it as hand-eye coordination.

he can interpret it at long range visually. The coordination of eye and hand movements, therefore, becomes an important indicator of the child's development of perceptual skills.

Getman uses the example of texture to illustrate this point. If while sitting in your seat you would look around at the various objects that you could see and thought of them in terms of texture, you would probably see objects that appear rough, smooth, bumpy, etc. On what do you base this judgment? You certainly did not feel all of those objects with your eyes. Obviously, therefore, these visual impressions are based on earlier tactual experiences such as touching these objects with your fingertips. Over a period of time by touching and observing such objects at the same time you were able to substitute your visual interpretation for your tactual interpretation so that you now have the ability to look at an object and determine its texture without touching it.

Following this example one step further we can observe the importance of movement to interpretations of texture. Place your finger on a piece of clothing you are wearing without moving it. What does this experience tell you about its texture? Now gently rub the same finger on the same piece of clothing. You probably found that movement does, indeed, enhance your knowledge of texture.

What about visual interpretation of size and shape and weight? Size and shape, for example, are considered so important that every test of intelligence and learning ability contain items about them. We are constantly making judgments concerning all of these factors visually—yet again, what are these judgments based on? Can you imagine trying to determine any of these qualities of an object without previously having had the opportunity to handle and move this or similar objects? In what terms could you describe such an object to another person if you had no prior experiences with the object on which to base your description?

This points up the importance of experienced-based perceptual learning in all communications. For two people to be able to communicate with each other they need to have had common visual and tactual experiences, or they simply will not be "speaking the same language."

Getman makes a strong plea for improved communication between physical educators and optometrists in the effort to reduce or eliminate learning difficulties in children. He points out that optometrists are making a determined effort to aid the motor development of children by encouraging the proper use of their visual systems as guidance mechanisms for both large muscle and fine motor movements. On the other hand, physical educators can contribute greatly to the development of vision through the proper development of fundamental motor skills in children. Getman has, therefore, concluded that the greatest contribution to the elimination of learning problems will have to come from physical educators. His challenge to this profession is quite clear:

> "What you do in the primary years can prevent more visual problems and distortions than can all the optometrists in practice. I hope you will realize that you can do more to prepare children for the academic demands now being placed upon them than can any other group of professionals available to children." (6, p. 27)

Critique

Now that we have a basic understanding of the theoretical concepts underlying perceptual-motor development, we should look at the evidence presented from an objective point of view. In his book, <u>Perceptual</u> and <u>Motor Development</u> in <u>Infants</u> and <u>Children</u> (1), Bryant J. Cratty has made a very critical analysis of perceptual-motor theory. He has concluded, based on the available research evidence, that many of the claims of perceptual-motor theorists have not been proven scientifically. Consequently, even though he believes that movement experiences are essential in the life of the maturing child, he rejects the notion that all learning is motor based.

Cratty's search through the neurological literature of the past 75 years led him to the conclusion that Delacato's theory of cerebral dominance is not supported by neurological research. He points out that complex motor actions have been traced to various parts of the brain and not just controlled by one hemisphere. Hand and eye preference seems to be more of an inherited trait rather than one determined by a dominant cerebral hemisphere. Another important factor in hand preference has been cultural pressure such as left-handers being "encouraged" for one reason or another to switch to using their right hands.

Cratty also indicates that having the dominant hand, foot, and eye on the same side of the body, which Delacato deems to be highly desirable, is not common.

Citing child development literature he points out that a number of visual abilities develop before the accurate development of many motor abilities. Ocular tracking, for example, may be efficient two full years before the child develops a perfect gait (walking pattern).

Delacato has suggested that in cases where children have "skipped" certain developmental stages, they should be manually guided through these stages by the parent or teacher. Cratty feels that in cases where this guided movement is done despite objections from the child, rather than aiding the child, great emotional harm may be done to him.

In other studies in which investigators have taken children through the developmental sequence suggested by Delacato (i.e., they crawl before they creep, etc.), results have not supported his assertions that such training will lead to higher I.Q.'s and an improvement in reading ability. Cratty also points out that a number of medical and health organizations have criticized Delacato's theories and methods as not being supported by research evidence.

Cratty summarizes the Delacato theories as being of possible value to severely retarded and brain-damaged children, but apparently of little help to normal children or slow learners in reading or other academic areas.

He rejects Kephart's theory that directionality stems from laterality by citing research which indicates that the ability to identify right and left body parts is not related to directionality in children with perceptual-motor problems. Kephart hypothesized that children with the inability to translate laterality information into space would reflect this inability in letter and word reversals, thereby handicapping them in reading. Cratty suggests that even if children do reverse letters, it may not be as crucial as Kephart and others have suspected.

Kephart's theory that motor learning underlies perceptual development appears to be contrary to existing evidence that motor learning is specific, or in other words not transferrable to other kinds of learning. Other studies indicate that evaluations of perceptual-motor abilities of young children do not relate to later intelligence. Indeed, a child may be as old as eight years of age before adult intelligence can be predicted with any accuracy. Thus, according to Cratty, Kephart's idea that early motor experiences influence later intellectual development cannot be supported by research findings.

Cratty next points out that Kephart's belief in the importance of visual tracking in academic success is opposed by a great deal of research which has been conducted over a period of many years. Kephart claims that the child's eyes should glide smoothly across the printed page, and if they do not, it is an indication of visual problems. Opposing research indicates that the child's eyes move too fast for conscious control and that rather than moving smoothly they move in rapid starts and stops across the page. This research has indicated that hyperopia (farsightedness) is more likely to be the visual factor in poor reading rather than tracking.

Finally, Cratty cites a number of studies in which the Kephart techniques of visual training and large muscle activities were applied to groups of poor readers while control groups were given reading practice, and in each case there was either no significant difference between groups or the control groups improved more in reading ability. (Chapter Three Part I of this book is devoted to what research has discovered about perceptual-motor development).

Cratty has, therefore, concluded that, in general, Kephart's techniques do not appear to lead to improved reading ability in normal children and children with reading problems. He does point out, however, that certain of Kephart's ideas do have merit. For example, he feels that Kephart's motor development program designed for neurologically impaired youngsters could be of value in improving motor functions. That is, certain motor abilities which are specifically trained for through Kephart's techniques do seem to improve. Due to lack of conclusive evidence one way or the other Cratty stresses that Kephart's theory that motor activities in the preschool years may prepare children for later learnings should not be totally discarded without further investigation.

Cratty is also quite critical of many of the claims of Getman. For example, Getman's belief that movement efficiency is basic to ocular functions and ultimately to academic success is not supported by available evidence, according to Cratty. It appears that the ability to read well is mainly dependent on the higher mental processes. Studies have consistently indicated I.Q. differences between good and poor readers. Therefore, Cratty suggests that because reading calls upon the use of both the eyes and the brain, it is probably the brain more than the eyes which will make the greatest contribution to the understanding of the printed page.

There does not seem to be a great deal of support for Getman's theory of a close relationship between ocular function and reading ability. Cratty cites two studies in which reading understanding and eye movements appear to have very little relationship to each other. In terms of reading speed Cratty feels that visual training to reduce the number of times the child's eyes come to rest per 100 words would not increase reading speed. Cratty points out that as children mature, they naturally read faster because they fix their eyes on fewer words. He feels, however, that visual training to decrease the number of fixations would defeat its own purpose because the child would have to fixate longer on each word his eyes came to rest on.

Again, Cratty points out that tracking ability is not related to reading ability. The number of times a child's eyes fix on a group of words, for example, seems to be inherited and relatively stable as the child matures. He suggests that efforts to train the eyes to function in some other manner appear to have little chance for success.

Cratty reviewed the existing research which supports Getman's theories and found it to be sparse and incomplete. Conversely, he points out that much research evidence exists which indicates that children with learning problems may have causes other than deficient eye function for their problems. Therefore, visual training such as that suggested by Getman should not be administered to large groups of children before more investigation into this area can be completed. Certainly no absolute statement can be made at this time concerning the role of visual training in ocular performance or on the role of ocular training in academic success.

To conclude his statement on Getman, Cratty emphasizes the probability that a number of children with learning problems do have visual problems. Thus, more extensive and efficient visual evaluations in the schools may lead to fewer learning problems. Finally, Cratty does not rule out the possibility that further research may prove many of Getman's theories to be correct.

Cratty summarizes his own feeling about the perceptual-motor area by writing:

> "I do not view perceptual-motor behavior, perceptual-motor learning or perceptual-motor training as either phrases to be avoided or supernatural cure-alls. Rather, I believe that the perceptions and related movements engaged in by human infants and children are important facets of their personalities. Perceptual and motor behavior are at times independent from each other and at other times may be joined in interesting ways. Most voluntary movement requires some kind of perceptual activity; the ball to be caught must first be watched, and smoothly executed complex movements are dependent on conscious or unconscious 'kinesthetic' feedback of previous components of claims of reactions." (1, p. 2)

However, despite his criticisms concerning these theories, Cratty also recognizes the contributions that movement behavior can make in the lives of children. In his book, Physical Expressions of Intelligence, he cites research studies and other supporting evidence in analyzing the significance of motor activity to intellectual development. He clarifies his position on this topic from both a theoretical and practical viewpoint. (2)

One very important point which has largely been overlooked is the potential for improving motor abilities of children through perceptual-motor programs. In our rush to connect improvement in motor skills with improvement in learning ability, we have neglected the fact that through perceptual-motor training programs many children with poor motor skills have greatly improved their motor performance. Consequently, if we believe in the worth and importance of the development of motor skills in the growth and development of young children, it would appear that perceptual-motor programs would be of great significance in the life of the child even if they did not lead to an improvement in reading or other cognitive areas.

Perceptual-motor theory may offer at least part of the answer to the problem of children with learning difficulties. As Cratty has warned, however, learning theory is only as strong as the research that backs it up. What, then, does research tell us about the applicability of perceptual-motor theory? Chapter Three will attempt to answer this question concerning not only children with learning problems but with slow learners and "normal" children as well.

Bibliography

1. Cratty, Bryant J. Perceptual and Motor Development in Infants and Children. London: The Macmillan Company, 1970

2. _____. Physical Expressions of Intelligence. New Jersey: Prentice-Hall, Inc., 1972.

3. Delacato, Carl H. The Diagnosis and Treatment of Speech and Reading Problems. Springfield, Illinois: Charles C. Thomas Publishers, 1963.

4. _____. The Treatment and Prevention of Reading Problems, Springfield, Illinois: Charles C. Thomas Publishers, 1959.

5. Flavell, John H. The Developmental Psychology of Jean Piaget, Princeton, New Jersey: D. Van Nostrand Company, Inc., 1963.

6. Getman, G.N. "Concerns of the Optometrist for Motor Development," Foundations and Practices in Perceptual-Motor Learning—A Quest for Understanding, Washington, D.C.: American Association for Health, Physical Education, and Recreation, 1971.

7. Hebb, D.O. The Organization of Behavior, New York: John Wiley & Sons, Inc., 1949.

8. Kephart, Newell C. The Slow Learner in the Classroom, Columbus, Ohio: Charles E. Merrill Publishing Company, 1960.

9. Piaget, Jean and Barbel Inhelder. The Psychology of the Child, New York: Basic Books, Inc., 1969.

10. Radler, D.H., and Newell C. Kephart. Success Through Play, New York: Harper & Row Publishers, 1960.

11. Wright, Logan. "Highlights of Human Development, Birth to Age Eleven," Perceptual-Motor Foundations: A Multidisciplinary Concern, Washington, D.C.: American Association for Health, Physical Education, and Recreation, 1969.

CHAPTER THREE

The Effectiveness
of Perceptual-Motor
Function: Fact or Fiction?

Whatever skeptic could inquire for,
For every why he had a wherefore
Samuel Butler

Within the past few years there has been an increasing interest in perceptual-motor function and its relationship to academic achievement in young children. Many psychologists and educators point out that children who have learning
problems in the classroom may also have poor motor ability. They believe that
by providing preschool and primary grade youngsters with experiences in perceptual-motor skills they are more likely to be free of the learning problems
which affect children who lack these perceptual-motor skills. If this is basically
true, then one must ask a more specific question; does perceptual-motor function serve as a foundation to help children to read and write as well as to think
abstractly? Unfortunately, there does not seem to be an answer as directly and
concretely as the question has been stated. Learning experts are, however, seeking to answer these and other related significant questions. But let us start from
the beginning. Can children be classified into groups which are most likely to
have perceptual-motor difficulties? Yes—they are mentally retarded children
and those of normal intelligence who still underachieve in the classroom. Children
who have normal intelligence and achievement are also being studied to determine
what role perceptual-motor function may have upon their progress. Each of these
groups should be examined closely.

Educable Mentally Retarded Children

There are different classifications of mental retardation, but many studies
in perceptual-motor learning deal with children who are classified as educable
mentally retarded (EMR). This basically means they are of below "average"
intelligence but still capable of attending public school.

In working with this classification of children, it is worthwhile to note their general inability to move well. For example, some EMR children may have difficulty when asked to name specific body parts or in locating themselves in relation to other objects. They may also be unable to tell the difference between the left and right side of their body. These kinds of observations have led interested workers to develop instruments which determine general intelligence through different measures of body awareness. These measures of body awareness have further led to the creation and use of perceptual-motor tasks in the educational programs for the EMR child. Teaching a variety of motor activities in these programs is considered to be an important educational tool for a number of reasons. There are necessary self care skills of life such as dressing and eating which must be mastered. Successful participation in games and sports skills can be very beneficial in helping the child to have a better feeling of self worth. It also takes skill to coordinate hand movements with vision in order to be successful in handwriting. Finally, there are experts who suggest that motor activities are useful to help EMR children by requiring thought processes similar to those necessary in various classroom activities. For example, learning to memorize the order of acts in a challenge course may help with the ability to place letters in the correct order in a word. However, much more research needs to be conducted to verify these and other beliefs about the role of motor activities for the educable mentally retarded.

Comparing Normal and EMR Children in Motor Development and Skill

Research indicates that EMR children are generally shorter in height, weigh less, and are inferior in motor skills when compared to children of the same age but of normal intelligence. It has been determined that normal children can usually score much higher than EMR children in such skills as standing on one foot, throwing a ball, running fast, and balancing a wand on the index finger. This trend is continued in other tasks such as pull-ups, the standing broad-jump, sit-ups, and running six hundred yards. In large muscle skills such as those just mentioned, it is estimated that EMR children are generally about two to four years behind normal children in performance.

EMR children are also usually inferior to normal children in skills which call for fine motor coordination. Where accuracy counts in such tasks as throwing objects at a target, or following the lines in a geometric pattern, they are less successful. In fact, as the fine motor task becomes more difficult their chances of success with it decrease. However, there is positive support for the belief that structured programs of physical activity can improve the motor performance of these children. This, of course, points out the need for activity which can serve as an important educational tool for them. Evidence indicates that many EMR children can, with proper help and practice, achieve normal levels of motor performance.

With this knowledge the course of action is clear for the physical educator who wishes to work with EMR youth. The activity program should be flexible and contain a wide variety of movement experiences designed to increase individual fitness and skill levels. Fine motor coordination skills are also valuable tools necessary for further learning.

Is There A Relationship Between Motor and Intellectual Ability?

This is a timely and very significant question. When considering some EMR children, it can be said that their I.Q.'s have improved after completing a regular program of physical activities. It should be mentioned, however, that such improvements are linked to activity programs which stress listening carefully to instructions as well as concentrating on specific given tasks. This kind of practice is almost certain to have a favorable effect upon those tested for any learning gains. That is, physical activities may help them to think about the nature of each particular classroom activity in terms of its sequence and variety.

The results of such programs is not always as favorable though. There are those EMR children lacking perceptual-motor skills who still do not improve their physical or mental abilities. The reason for this may be because they are more secure and have better self-concepts than other EMR children. This may partially explain their lack of any noted progress. This also emphasizes the possibility that improvement in motor skills, which may result in greater classroom achievement, may be due to a better self-concept brought about by more successful skill performance.

To answer the question above more directly, some investigators have found a slight relationship between I.Q. and motor ability. Also, they believe that the specific items of coordination and balance have a greater relationship to intelligence than other motor abilities. In fact, balancing ability can differ significantly between EMR and normal children. The general feeling of experts working in this area then, is that intelligence and motor ability are definitely related to some extent. Nevertheless, it is difficult to prove that perceptual-motor function is directly responsible for improving the learning ability of EMR children. When gains in learning have been observed, the physical activities used in the training program were similar to those tasks and skills which were included in the achievement tests. This probably created a "learning effect." It is also true that the extra personal attention and praise given the child in a perceptual-motor program generally has a favorable effect upon learning improvement. Nevertheless, these significant learning increases, which occurred after planned activity programs, are interesting and noteworthy. It appears that when a perceptual-motor task is closely related to a specific learning skill, it is possible for the child to improve learning in that skill, provided he has enough practice over a period of time. When a child is learning to recognize and draw geometric figures, then the perceptual-motor task should be concerned with activities which reflect this in as many similar ways as possible. It is highly doubtful that a large muscle activity such as skipping will teach the EMR child to recognize and duplicate the geometric figures. This does not mean that skipping is not important to the child's total welfare, but motor activities such as skipping, running and hopping appear to have little effect on his ability to understand something as specific as recognizing and copying geometric forms.

The teacher who has a special interest in working with educable mentally retarded children has an opportunity to play an important part in their education. Physical activity should be integrated into their daily lives for a variety of organic, social, and emotional reasons. Much more study needs to be done, however if we are to fully understand what contributions perceptual-motor programs can make to the intellectual development and welfare of these children. Thus far the contributions appear to be very promising.

Normal Children

Most of the research completed in perceptual-motor function has been largely concerned with educable mentally retarded children. However, recent attention has also been given to trying to understand the role of perceptual-motor function in learning with normal children.

The Relationship Between Intelligence and Motor Development

During the first years of a child's life, some experts believe there may be a relationship between intelligence and motor development. In fact, tests of general intelligence are largely made up of motor items for children under two years of age. It is generally believed that babies who are abnormally slow in learning to sit, stand, or walk are also usually slow in intellectual development. Those children who show early development in motor skills usually develop intellectually at a faster pace than would a child who shows average development. It would be logical then to associate a high level of intelligence in older children with a high degree of motor coordination. Usually, however, this is not true. Many times very bright children are poorly coordinated in sports skills and activities requiring manual dexterity such as painting or sewing. Even though they are capable of developing these skills they probably do not really want to. Their interest lies in other activities in which motor skills do not play a personally important role. As a result, they are not motivated to practice them. Then, when compared to children their own age, they seem to be uncoordinated. When compared to children a couple of years older, with whom they come into contact during school, they seem to appear even more uncoordinated.

Intelligence and Motor Performance

With older children and adolescents, there does not seem to be a relationship between intelligence and motor performance. Even with children in the third and fourth grade there is little connection between their intellectual ability and success on a series of perceptual-motor tasks. Perhaps the best relationship between perceptual-motor skills and verbal learning takes place in early childhood. With age, achievement becomes more specific to the particular task and does not necessarily depend upon general motor skills. Take a general motor skill such as galloping for example. This does not seem to directly help the child to better control the movements of his pencil when learning to write. In this instance, it would be best to give the child practice in those skills which are specifically needed for handwriting.

However, primary school aged children show surprising positive relationships between perceptual-motor proficiency and intellectual ability. There also appears to be a positive relationship between perceptual-motor proficiency and academic achievement. A child's ability to identify his body parts is a very good predictor of intelligence and academic achievement. A word of caution is in order here though.

We must remember that the relationship between perceptual-motor proficiency to intellectual ability and academic achievement does not mean that a direct relationship exists. That is, if an intelligent child has a superior degree of motor skill as opposed to a less intelligent child who has poor motor skill, the cause for this would not necessarily be due to the differences in their physical ability.

Perceptual-Motor Function and Reading

For a child, the task of learning to read can be a difficult one. Being able to read successfully involves such complex acts as recognizing and interpreting various symbols. Much evidence exists which points out how important it is for a child to have good visual skills necessary for successful reading ability. In 1953 Newell C. Kephart attempted to determine just what kind of visual skills pupils in grades three through twelve had. After testing 2200 children, he concluded that approximately four out of every ten children had visual skills below the level required for good schoolwork. He also discovered that the children who saw well worked well in school, and those who could not see well did poorly.

More recently, a total of 1510 children in the first three grades were studied. Each child was shown certain forms such as a circle, square, and triangle. They were told to draw them exactly as they saw the forms. The copying performance of each child was rated and checked against his school achievement. It was found that this test of visual skill was closely related to school achievement. That is, those children who copied the forms most accurately were generally found to achieve better in school.

One specific visual skill possibly related to reading success deals with how well the child can follow a moving object with his eyes. This is known as tracking ability. Examples are catching a ball in flight or watching a moving object swinging back and forth on a string. How well a child can do these kinds of tasks may generally indicate his reading success at a later time. Tests of motor coordination which involve large muscle movements as well as tests using more controlled and accurate muscle movements may also be useful in pointing out future reading success. Basic testing principles such as those just mentioned have been used to study what effect an experimental physical education program has upon reading readiness and the ability to understand what is seen. In a physical education program, such activities as imitating movements (Simon says), directionality (an awareness of left, right, up and down, etc., in space) moving various body parts at the same time such as the right arm and left leg while lying on the back (Angels-in-the-Snow) and related program ideas such as balance and spatial awareness (small, large, etc.) have been used. Activities such as these can possibly help young children in reading readiness and the ability to understand what is seen.

Underachieving Children

There are many children in school that are classified as having normal intelligence but, for unknown reasons, are achieving far below their intended grade level. There is not very much known about how perceptual-motor function affects the underachieving child. Of what is known, however, the results appear encouraging.

For example, improvements in the reading ability of primary grade pupils after participating in perceptual-motor training programs have been found. Activities in these programs consisted of walking the balance beam, throwing and catching skills, jumping rope, locomotor movements and practice in directionality.

More positive results were found with two children who were well below their grade levels in reading (46). In order to increase their reading ability, they received ten months of perceptual-motor training. The activities were based upon the following general areas:

1. Large muscle activities—hopping and bouncing a ball.
2. Body Schema—balance, directionality.
3. Form perception—reproducing designs such as a triangle or rectangle.
4. Fine motor skill activities—marbles, jacks, pick-up sticks and tracing.
5. Visualization—drawing a map or describing trips and scenes.
6. Visual-motor coordination—batting a ball.
7. Visual synthesis—putting a jigsaw puzzle together.
8. Conceptualization—sustained sequential thinking (logical ordering of numbers, events) cause and effect reasoning and imagining what future events would be like.

After this extensive program both children achieved above their present grade levels. This program was judged to be effective because it was geared to individual levels which permitted each child to work with visual symbols. It was also believed that the program was helpful in rebuilding their sense of self-confidence. Similar gains have also been noted in culturally different children.

One important question to ask at this point is, how can reading gains occur when actual reading skills are not taught? The explanation for this may rest with the belief that greater self-control is increased in the child which permits him to read and answer questions more carefully. Many of the activities in a perceptual-motor program emphasize that the child focus his attention upon accurate listening and looking. This way the child develops, through the medium of activity, a greater capacity for learning which is based upon better concentration. The child still needs to be taught actual reading skills and content though. A second related factor may be due to the increased personal attention given to the child. This, in connection with a successful experience in physical activities, may enhance the child's feeling of self-worth which in turn permits him to achieve success.

Some Implications of Perceptual-Motor Research

Based upon her review of research, Hope Smith (52) has presented some very readable information for teachers who are interested in perceptual-motor function and teaching children. She reminds us that these implications are only speculative in nature, and they need to be evaluated in a teaching-learning situation using necessary research procedures. Nevertheless, they are discussed here in order to further stimulate thinking about the topic.

Vision

Young children are farsighted until about the age of six or seven. Therefore, when working with preschool and primary grade children on throwing and catching skills, some specific steps should be taken. When throwing at a wall target, for example, make it large enough to be seen clearly. If the child is throwing at a relatively small target, it will probably be seen best at a distance of six feet or closer. Items such as bean bags, balls and blocks are probably seen better if they are not extremely small. When throwing an object for the child to catch, be sure to throw it as slowly as possible. That way, the child's eyes will have time to focus upon the approaching object.

When identifying and classifying objects, three and four-year-olds generally rely upon their shape or form rather than upon the colors of the objects. At about age five color becomes more important than form. By age six or seven color and shape are used in classifying and telling differences among and between objects. The color blue is favored by both boys and girls with red and orange as a second choice. Yellow appears to be the color least favored. Knowing this, it may be a good idea to include more variety and complexity in play objects and equipment for three and four-year-olds. Color is not that important. If working with five-year-olds, however, a wide variety of colors could be introduced into their surroundings and toys. This may be a critical time in which motivation can be increased for motor performance through the use of colors. In the first through third grades, it may be possible to make physical education class more educational and exciting by using a wide variety of shapes and colors in objects used for play.

Figure-ground phenomenon is the ability to visually pick out and see a simple figure or object in a complex background. An example of this would be an outfielder visually following a pop fly ball against the background of the crowd. This ability to find an object in the complex ground is a slow developmental process which reaches its peak in the teens. Both boys and girls reach their top levels of proficiency at about fourteen to sixteen years of age. Then, however, girls begin a gradual reduction in this ability to about age twenty or twenty-one at which time a leveling-off period occurs. Boys have a tendency to keep the level of performance they have established at approximately age fourteen to sixteen until age twenty or twenty-one. Then there is a slight decrease in performance before the leveling-off period. Younger children show less ability than older children in this phenomenon, and girls have less ability than boys at each age level. If children do poorly for their age and sex on this visual task, they are said to be field-dependent. If they do well on the task, they are field-independent. Based upon this knowledge, poor motor performance by individuals in activities which require striking and catching may be because they are visually field-dependent. The physical education teacher should be alert to this possibility and select a proper course of action to help those with this difficulty. With the right kind of practice, it is possible to increase one's ability in figure-ground performance.

Depth perception and size constancy are learned visual abilities which develop gradually as children mature. Depth perception is the ability to visually determine the distance of an object from the observer. Size constancy is the ability to see and recognize the actual size of an object regardless of other things that may change its apparent size. An example of this might be that since we know what a standard size football is like, it will still be the same size to us even though we may move away from it a distance of 50 yards.

The implications of knowing these facts are important. Having adequate depth perception is essential when performing a variety of motor skills. For children, it is important to offer as many situations as possible which give them practice in depth perception and size constancy.

Phi phenomenon (autokinetic movement) is a visual illusion that gives us the notion that a stationary object is in motion. This can happen if we focus our eyes on an object for a long period of time.

In some activities the child may be required to maintain constant focus with his eyes on a specific object or spot. A balance beam routine may demand this. If so, the child should be told to periodically look away from the object or spot just a few degrees to the left or right. This can prevent the phi phenomenon and may help the child perform more efficiently.

Retinal inhibition is the term used to describe the fact that in some cases a person may not "see" an object even though he may have 20/20 vision. The intent here is not to describe the physiological process that causes this phenomenon to happen, but rather to just mention that it does occur. The teacher should give more than just auditory instructions when giving pupils visual direction cues related to motor performance. For example, after giving the pupils verbal directions for throwing a ball at one of many wall targets placed side by side, it would also be a good idea to provide visual direction by walking up to and touching the desired target.

Audition (Hearing)

Many studies indicate that human babies experience some sound sensations before birth. Of course, as soon as a baby is born, he experiences a variety of sounds which continue throughout his developmental years and beyond. Industrial studies have shown that high noise, heat, and humidity levels in the working environment may be directly related to decreased production rates. Therefore, it is important to create a proper teaching-learning environment in physical education if possible. Indoor facilities should be equipped with acoustical materials and room temperature levels should be at appropriate levels to accommodate the rise in body temperature brought about by vigorous activity.

Auditory figure-ground ability involves detecting one specific sound within an entire complexity of sound. To illustrate, when listening to a symphony orchestra, a person can pick out the clarinets as they play simultaneously with all of the other instruments. This depends upon a person's listening training which would vary greatly with different people.

The implication for teachers of physical education may be that auditory training should begin early and continue in the activity program. Surfaces of walls, floors, and other objects can be of different materials which would produce various sounds when associated with different activities. When planned for, these can be used as cues to one's motor performance. The sound of a well-hit baseball, for example, can be one of the first cues to the player concerning the success of his performance.

Information related to directionality of sound indicates that people have a tendency to begin their movements in the direction from which the sound cue was given. That is, if a verbal cue is given instructing a person to move a body part or parts to the left, but the verbal cue comes from the right side of the person, the tendency will be to move first to the right before going to the left. An awareness is important to both the beginner and the advanced pupil when learning physical skills. Thus, when the pupil is working on a specific direction in which he is to respond, the teacher should be sure that he gives the sound cue from the direction in which the movement is to be made.

Auditory rhythm perception is:

"... the identification of a regulated series of sounds interspersed by regulated movements of silence in repeated patterns. It also involves tempo and accent (increased amplitude at regulated moments in the pattern)." (52, p. 32)

An example of this could be clapping a three-quarter time rhythm with an accent on the first note followed by two more notes within the measure. This is followed by a measure of silence. Then, repeat the same rhythm followed by another measure of silence. This pattern can be repeated as many times as one wishes. Being able to listen to a rhythm and then repeat it is a complex process involving a sense of time developed through hearing. To further clarify this, consider a teacher with a class of pupils. He could play a record that has a specific rhythm interspersed with periods of silence. He then would ask the class to listen carefully to the rhythm of the music and try to "feel it." They could then listen to the rhythm again as the teacher claps in time with the rhythm. Next the class could clap in time with the rhythm while watching the teacher who is leading them in the clapping. At this point the class is involved with music which has a definite rhythm and pattern as perceived through their auditory and visual senses. Studies have shown that children start to make time discriminations in music through the auditory mode before the visual mode. That is, they can hear and understand a measure of music sooner than they can read and understand a measure of music. Being able to hear and understand the music aids in helping them read and understand it.

The physical education program can serve as an important medium which can provide auditory experiences in rhythms. This, combined with motor experiences, can be a valuable asset to the total development of the child.

Tactile Perception (Touch)

In young children the end organs of touch in the skin appear to develop in a cephalocaudal pattern. Receptors in the area of the head and upper limbs develop before the lower limb receptors. Thus, development goes from the top portions of the body to the lower portions of the body, or in a cephalocaudal pattern. The mouth and tongue contain many tactile end organs which the child uses to explore objects during the first couple of years of life. The mouth, tongue, fingers and palms of the hands, toes and soles of the feet are the most sensitive parts of the body. Both sides of the trunk of the body are less sensitive than other body parts because there are not as many end organs of touch located here.

Children should be given many chances to explore their environment tactilely using various body parts. Activities which involve the trunk area of the body should be part of the physical education program. Log rolls, forward and backward rolls, and sliding head and feet first on both sides of the body are such examples. Aquatics can also be useful for providing many tactile experiences. Gravitational force is minimal and the pressure of the water against the body and extremities is very evident.

Tennis shoes, as valuable as they are to necessary safety, have a tendency to "mask" a child's sense of feeling in his feet. It would be advantageous for children to perform some of their physical activities without shoes. The tactile receptors on the bottom of the feet serve to signal to the child a shifting body weight as well as indicating differences in surface textures.

Providing different kinds of tactile experiences through the environment receives little attention in our physical education programs. Play areas could be divided and surfaced with various textures such as sand, cement, natural grass, plastic, and black-top.

Balance Mechanisms (Inner Ear)

Motion sickness is an uncommon occurrence in children under two years of age because organic development of the inner ear is not quite complete. The balance mechanisms, in conjunction with vision and the sense of touch, and knowing where our body parts are help us to understand the relationship of our body in space. During activities which require spinning, such as in ice skating, dizziness can be controlled by fixing the eyes on one spot while turning.

Including spinning types of activities in the physical education program and teaching children to focus on one spot can help them reduce vertigo, or a feeling of dizziness. Such activities might include spinning around on gym scooters, or playing various forms of merry-go-round using hula hoops, ropes or gym scooters.

Proprioception
(Muscle, tendon, and joint senses which tell a person the position and movements of parts of his body; this is also known as kinesthetic sense)

When teaching a child how to kick a soccer ball for the first time, the teacher may tell him to try and "feel" the movement. This kinesthetic or "muscle sense" is important when learning a new skill. The pupil must be aware of what his muscles are doing when performing a physical activity. Studies show there is no general kinesthetic sense, but it is more specific to that part of the body involved in the skill. A test of kinesthesis would be to blindfold a person and have him place a mark on a target in as close to a specific spot as possible, when given a verbal cue. Balance is also an important factor of kinesthesis. This "muscle sense" plays an important part in skill learning and can be improved through practice. For example, if a person practiced a skill blindfolded such as the baseball swing, he would tend to rely upon his kinesthetic sense which would probably improve.

A Need for More Investigation

Now having taken a closer look at the effectiveness of perceptual-motor learning and some of its implications, the teacher should consider some timely problems which are uniquely related to this topic. Perceptual-motor theories of learning are only theories which must be further studied and developed if they are to serve their intended purpose. B. R. Carlson (6) has identified some problems in perceptual-motor learning which need further thought and investigation.

He points out that many tests exist for determining intelligence and personality, but how many perceptual-motor tests are there which have been designed by physical educators? The most popular tests in use today have been developed by an occupational therapist, psychologists, and one physical educator. Most of these test makers are psychologists who have used movement as a basis for their test items. Because of the professional background of these individuals, it is difficult for a physical educator to choose an item in their tests and determine for certain what it measures. For example, in one test the letters "m" and "n" are placed on the chalkboard for the child to duplicate. If the child fails this task, it could be for any number of reasons. However, only a single score is recorded for this test making it very difficult, if not impossible, to identify the problem and how extensive it may be. This is why the physical educator needs to be concerned about better understanding these kinds of items found in the stated example, as well as developing additional perceptual-motor tests. Another related problem is that many tests today are subjectively evaluated by the person giving the test. This means that a personal judgment is made as to how a child is performing in relation to his age. The problem here is that some people may not be adequate judges because they are not that familiar with normal perceptual-motor development. A solution to this problem is to develop norms gathered from a large sample of children. Then one child's test scores can be more accurately compared against the scores of many other children who are of the same age. In using such an approach, it will be possible to have a better understanding of the child and the level at which he is functioning.

Another area needing more thought is visual perception. Remember that this is more than just the ability to see accurately. Visual perception also involves being able to interpret and make sense out of what one sees as well. If a child does not have 20/20 vision, this can be helped by prescribing glasses or through corrective surgery. However, there are those children with 20/20 vision who have such problems as reversing their letters when writing or not being able to remember a sequence of numbers or letters they have seen. These kinds of problems cause the child to have difficulty learning in the classroom. Physical educators need to identify those perceptual-motor activities which are vital for the normal development of visual perception and what they do.

If medical doctors find that there is nothing organically wrong with a child's eyes, he should then be helped by the optometrist or physical educator. Professionals in optometry have been urging the physical education profession to take a more active interest in problems of this nature for years. However, our knowledge has not kept pace with the problems in this area.

The problem of how long the effects of perceptual-motor learning stay with the child is another area that needs to be considered. What are the long-term effects of this type of training? Just how vital is it for a person to have what is considered to be normal perceptual-motor function?

Another problem needing attention is how does perceptual-motor training relate to academic learning? The placing of events in their proper order in the classroom is very important to success. Reading calls for this proper ordering and following verbal directions also requires it. It may be very possible to further this ability through physical activity. A series of physical tasks or movements could be presented verbally or by demonstration depending upon the particular deficit of the child. This may help him arrange words in their proper order or write letters of a word in the order they should appear.

Carlson also asks if physical education should be concerned about helping mentally and physically handicapped children. He makes the observation that physical education has been geared largely toward the normal and physically gifted person. He feels, however, that the physical education profession has the expertise to make a significant contribution in the area of perceptual-motor learning.

There is a need to understand much more about the nature of perceptual-motor function in relation to academic achievement in children. What is known about this area, although opinions and findings vary, appears encouraging and certainly warrants further investigation. Only in this manner can the role and scope of perceptual-motor function be fully realized. The physical education profession is in a very favorable position to carry out the role of perceptual-motor function and to help determine its total worth to the elementary school child.

Bibliography

1. Argenti, R.M. "The Effects of Systematic Motor Training on Selected Perceptual-Motor Attributes of Mentally Retarded Children." Unpublished Dissertation, The University of Tennessee, 1968.

2. Ball, T.S. and W.E. Wilsoncroft. "Perceptual-Motor Deficits and the Phi Phenomenon; cerebral palsied mentally retarded children." American Journal of Mental Deficiency, March 1967, 71, 797-800.

3. Bell, R.J., et al. "Perceptual-Motor Program Produces Positive Results; Farmington State Hospital School, Missouri." School and Community, November 1969, 56, 17.

4. Black, A.H. and L.J. Davis. "Relationship Between Intelligence and Sensorimotor Proficiency in Retardates." American Journal of Mental Deficiency, July 1966, 71, 55-59.

5. Cantor, G. and C. Stacey. "Manipulative Dexterity in Mental Defectives." American Journal of Mental Deficiency, 1951, 56, 401-410.

6. Carlson, B.R. "Status of Research on Children with Perceptual-Motor Dysfunction." Journal of Health, Physical Education, and Recreation, April 1972, 43, 57-59.

7. Chasey, W.C. and W. Wyrick. "Effect of a gross motor development program on form perception skills of educable retarded children." Research Quarterly, October 1970, 41, 345.

8. Clifton, M. "A Developmental Approach to Perceptual-Motor Experiences." Journal of Health, Physical Education, and Recreation, April 1970, 41, 34.

9. Cratty, B.J. "Some Perceptual-Motor Attributes of Mentally Retarded Children and Youth." California Journal of Educational Research, September 1967, 18, 188-193.

10. _____ and Sister Margaret Mary Martin. Perceptual-Motor Efficiency in Children. Philadelphia: Lea and Febiger, 1969.

11. _____. Movement Behavior and Motor Learning. Philadelphia: Lea and Febiger, 1964.

12. Cronback, L.J. Essentials of Psychological Testing. New York: Harper and Row, 1960.

13. Cruickshank, W.M. and G.O. Johnson. Education of Exceptional Children and Youth. New Jersey: Prentice-Hall, 1958.

14. Dunham, P. "Teaching Motor Skills to the Mentally Retarded." Exceptional Children, May 1969, 35, 739-744.

15. Dunn, L.M. (ed.) Exceptional Children in the Schools. New York: Holt, Rinehart and Winston, 1963.

16. Edgar, C.L. "Perceptual-Motor Training as an Aid to Development of Reading Abilities." Claremont Reading Conference Yearbook, 1967, 31, 219-228.

17. Emmons, C.A. "A Comparison of Selected Gross-Motor Activities of the Getman-Kane and the Kephart Perceptual-Motor Training Programs and Their Effects Upon Certain Readiness Skills of First-Grade Negro Children." Unpublished Dissertation, The Ohio State University, 1968.

18. Fisher, K.L. "Effects of Perceptual-Motor Training on the Educable Mentally Retarded." Exceptional Children, November 1971, 38, 264-266.

19. Footlik, S.W. "Perceptual-Motor Training and Cognitive Achievement: A Survey of the Literature." Journal of Learning Disabilities, January 1970, 3, 40-43.

20. Francis R.J. and G.L. Rarick. "Motor Characteristics of the Mentally Retarded." American Journal of Mental Deficiency, 1959, 63, 792-811.

21. Green, C. and E. Ziegler. "Social Deprivation and the Performance of Retarded and Normal Children on a Satiation Type Task." Child Development, 1962, 33, 499-508.

22. Guthrie, D.W. "A Study to Develop a Perceptual-Motor Screening Test for a Typical Child." Unpublished Dissertation, Brigham Young University, 1971.

23. Guyette, A., et al. "Some Aspects of Space Perception in Mental Retardates." American Journal of Mental Deficiency, 1964, 69, 90-100.

24. Howe, C.E. "A Comparison of Motor Skills of Mentally Retarded and Normal Children." Exceptional Children, 1959, 25, 352-354.

25. Hurlock, E.B. Child Development. New York: McGraw-Hill Book Company, 1964.

26. Ismail, A.H., J. Kane and D.R. Kirkendall. "Relationships Among Intellectual and Non-intellectual Variables." Research Quarterly, March 1969, 40, 83-92.

27. Kalakian, L.H. "Predicting Academic Achievement from Perceptual-Motor Efficiency in Educable Mentally Retarded Children." Unpublished Dissertation, University of Utah, 1971.

28. Kelly, T. and B.R. Amble. "I.Q. and Perceptual-Motor Scores as Predictors of Achievement Among Retarded Children." Journal of School Psychology, 1970, 8, No. 2, 99-102.

29. Kiphard, E. "Behavioral Integration of Problem Children Through Remedial Physical Education." Journal of Health, Physical Education, and Recreation, April 1970, 41, 45.

30. Kral, P.A. "Motor Characteristics and Development of Retarded Children: Success Experience." Education and Training of the Mentally Retarded, February 1972, 7, 14-21.

31. Liese, J.E. and H.A. Lerch, "The Relationship Between Physical Fitness and Intelligence in Trainable Mental Retardates." Presented at the American Association for Health, Physical Education, and Recreation Convention, Minneapolis, Minnesota, 1972.

32. Lietz, E.S. "An Investigation of the Perceptual-Motor Abilities of the Economically Disadvantaged Kindergarten Child as Compared to the Advantaged Kindergarten Child." Unpublished Dissertation, Southern Illinois University, 1968.

33. Lipton, E.D. "Perceptual-Motor Development Program's Effect on Visual Perception and Reading Readiness of First Grade Children." Research Quarterly, October 1970, 41, 402-405.

34. Little, S.J. "An Investigation of the Relationships Between Perceptual-Motor Proficiency, Intelligence and Academic Achievement in a Population of Normal Third-Grade Children." Unpublished Dissertation, University of Maryland, 1970.

35. Malpass, L.F. "Motor Proficiency in Institutionalized and Non-Institutionalized Retarded Children and Normal Children." American Journal of Mental Deficiency, 1960, 64, 1012-1015.

36. Matthews, W.H. "An Investigation of a Perceptual-Motor and Body Awareness Training Program with Culturally Limited Kindergarten Age Children." Unpublished Dissertation, The University of Tennessee, 1971.

37. McCormick, .C., et al. "Improvement in Reading Achievement Through Perceptual-Motor Training." Research Quarterly, October 1968, 39, 627-633.

38. McRaney, K.A. "A Study of Perceptual-Motor Exercises Utilized as an Early Grade Enrichment Program for the Improvement of Learning Activity and Motor Development." Unpublished Dissertation, University of Southern Mississippi, 1970.

39. Musgrove, D.M. "A Factor Analytic Study of Perceptual-Motor Attributes as Measured by Selected Test Batteries." Unpublished Dissertation, University of Northern Colorado, 1971.

40. O'Connor, C.M. "The Effects of Physical Activities Upon Motor Ability, Perceptual Ability, and Academic Achievement of First Graders." Unpublished Dissertation, The University of Texas, 1968.

41. Oliver, J.N. "The Effect of Physical Conditioning Exercises and Activities on the Mental Characteristics of Educationally Subnormal Boys." British Journal of Educational Psychology, 1958, 28, 155-164.

42. Plack, J.J. "An Evaluation of the Purdue Perceptual-Motor Survey as a Predictor of Academic and Motor Skills." Unpublished Dissertation, University of Minnesota, 1970.

43. Radler, D.H., and Newell C. Kephart. Success Through Play. New York: Harper and Row, 1960.

44. Roach, E.G. and Newell C. Kephart. The Purdue Perceptual-Motor Survey. Columbus, Ohio. Charles C. Merrill Co., 1966.

45. School District of the City of Pontiac. "The Effects of Perceptual-Motor Training on Perceptual and Reading Ability." Michigan: Department of Physical Education, Athletics and Recreation, February, 1966.

46. Seiderman, A.S. "A Look at Perceptual-Motor Training." Academic Therapy, Spring, 1972, 7, 315-321.

47. Silverstein, A.B., et al. "Clinical Assessment of Visual Perceptual Abilities in the Mentally Retarded." American Journal of Mental Deficiency, January 1970, 74, 524-526.

48. Singer, R.N. "Interrelationship of Physical, Perceptual-Motor, and Academic Achievement Variables in Elementary School Children." Perceptual and Motor Skills, 1967, 24, 967-890.

49. _____. Motor Learning and Human Performance. London: The Macmillan Co., 1968.

50. Sloan, W. "Motor Proficiency and Intelligence." American Journal of Mental Deficiency, 1951, 55, 394-406.

51. Smith, H.M. "Motor Activity and Perceptual Development; Some Implications for Physical Educators." Journal of Health, Physical Education and Recreation, February 1968, 39, 28-33.

52. _____. "Implications for Movement Education Experiences Drawn From Perceptual-Motor Research." Journal of Health, Physical Education and Recreation, April 1970, 41, 30-33.

53. Smith, P. "Perceptual-Motor Skills and Reading Readiness of Kindergarten Children." Journal of Health, Physical Education, and Recreation, April 1970, 41, 43.

54. Swanson, R.G. "A Study of the Relationship Between Perceptual-Motor Skills and the Learning of Word Recognition." Unpublished Dissertation, University of South Carolina, 1968.

55. Tidgewell, L. "Motor-Perceptual Development: A Base for Reading?" Claremont Reading Conference Yearbook, 1967, 31, 229-235.

56. Trussell, E.M. "Relation of Performance of Selected Physical Skills to Perceptual Aspects of Reading Readiness in Elementary School Children." Research Quarterly, May 1969, 40, 383-390.

57. Upchurch, W.B. "The Relationship Between Perceptual-Motor Skills and Word Recognition Achievement at the Kindergarten Level." Unpublished Dissertation, Syracuse University, 1971.

58. Weimer, W.R. "A Perceptuomotor and Oral Language Program for Children Identified as Potential Failures." Unpublished Dissertation, The University of New Mexico, 1971.

59. Wimsatt, W.R. "The Effect of Sensory-Motor Training on the Learning Abilities of Grade School Children." Unpublished Dissertation, University of Minnesota, 1966.

PART II
Screening for Perceptual-Motor Difficulties

> There are two ways of spreading light: to be
> the candle or the mirror that reflects it.
>   Edith Wharton

On finding children in class like Johnny and his friends who are having learning problems what can the teacher do? Based on information discussed in previous chapters, it is hoped that the teacher would try to determine if these children have a motor and/or perceptual basis for their problems. To assist in this task a very basic elementary screening test has been included. By administering this test to children with learning problems the teacher may find an indication of possible motor and/or perceptual connection with their problems. It should be emphasized that these are simplified measures and should be followed by more specific and thorough testing.

In interpreting the results of these screening devices, it is possible that a child may do poorly and still not have a perceptual-motor problem. Classroom performance, test results and teacher evaluation should all be used in determining the needs of the child. If at this point, there appears to be evidence for referral, then the teacher should use the team approach as outlined in Part III, Chapter One.

There are many things which the teacher can do with the child in the classroom or on the playground. If the child fails an item on the large muscle test, the teacher can use developmental activities for that area. The developmental activities in Part Three, Chapter Two, are divided according to the test items. In addition several programs, teaching aids, films, filmstrips, records and books are reviewed in the appendices. The purpose and method for ordering are included for the reader's convenience.

Large Muscle Screening Instrument

A. Materials

    1. Balance Beam*
    2. Playground ball—8 to 10 inches
    3. Chair

B. The score for each item is yes or no.

    1. <u>Balance</u> (static)   Yes   No   Comments

        Stand on one foot ten seconds (Examiner asks child to stand on one foot as long as possible. Then child is asked to stand on other foot.)

        <u>Yes</u> if child stands on either foot ten seconds. <u>No</u> if child fails to stand on either foot ten seconds.

    2. <u>Balance</u> (dynamic)   Yes   No   Comments

        Walk five feet on a balance beam without losing balance and touching floor.
        (Examiner asks child to walk the balance beam from one end to the other end.)

        <u>Yes</u> if child walks a distance of five feet without losing balance and touching floor.
        <u>No</u> if child fails to walk five feet without losing balance.

    3. <u>Coordination—Hand-eye</u>   Yes   No   Comments

        Child throws ball into air (slightly above head level) and catches it after one bounce, 2 out of 3 times.

        <u>Yes</u> if child catches balls 2 out of 3 times when thrown in air slightly above head.
        <u>No</u> if child fails to catch ball 2 out of 3 times or if ball is not thrown above head.

---

*If a balance beam is not available, a two-inch board or a painted line on the floor may be used.

4. Coordination—Hand-foot   Yes   No   Comments

Child drops ball from waist high and contacts
ball with foot 2 out of 3 times.

Yes if child touches ball with foot.
No if child fails to make contact with the ball.

5. Coordination—Symmetrical   Yes   No   Comments

Child lying on the floor in supine position is
asked to move arms and legs to side and return. It is recommended that the word right
and left not be used since many children will
not know right and left. The examiner may ask
child to move arm closest to some object
such as examiner, chalkboard, or door.

a. Slide one arm overhead and return.

b. Slide one leg to side and return.

c. Slide arm and leg on same side to the
    side and return

d. Slide arm on one side and leg on other
    side to the side and return

Yes if child is successful in moving the designated part without extraneous movement in 3
out of 4 of the directions.
No if child moves body parts other than those
designated by the examiner in more than one
of the 4 directions.

6. Space and direction   Yes   No   Comments

Child is given verbal directions to move
through space in a designated manner. (Chair
is placed 8-10 feet from child.)

a. Walk to the chair and touch it.

b. Stand so the chair is in front of you.

c. Stand so the chair is at your side.

Yes if the child moves as designated 3 out of
3 times.
No if child fails to touch chair or stand as
directed in relation to chair (in front or to
side).

7. Body Image

	Yes	No	Comments

Child is asked to touch selected body parts. This is a suggested list, the list may vary depending on age and experience of child:

Head	Eye
Foot	Knee
Leg	Nose
Ear	Arm
Elbow	Finger

<u>Yes</u> if child is successful in touching 8 out of 10 of the selected body parts.
<u>No</u> if child fails to touch the exact part, that is, he touches hand for finger, or if he fails to touch the correct part 8 out of 10 times.

C. Suggested Scoring Sheet

Large Muscle Screening

Name _____

	Yes	No	Comments
1. Balance—One Foot Stand			
2. Balance—Balance Beam Walk			
3. Coordination—Hand-eye			
4. Coordination—Hand-foot			
5. Coordination—Symmetrical—Angels in the Snow			
6. Space and Direction—Verbal Directions Touching			
7. Body Image—Touching Body Parts			

Fine Muscle Screening Instrument

A. Materials

1. Paper and pencil for each child
2. Blackboard and chalk
3. Pattern of a square
4. Sweater to button (shirt, dress, etc.)
5. Lined paper and scissors

B. The score for each item is yes or no.

1. Copying a square

	Yes	No	Comments

    Child is given paper and pencil and shown a square. He is asked to draw one like it. (It is recommended that the word "square" not be used.) If child is hesitant, examiner should draw a square and ask child to make one like it.

    Yes, if the square has four well defined angles and four sides which are approximately equal.
    No, if the square is not acceptable.

2. Buttoning

	Yes	No	Comments

    Examiner buttons a sweater and then asks child to button it.

    Yes, if the child can button.
    No, if he cannot button

3. Drawing a straight line

	Yes	No	Comments

    Child is asked to draw a line connecting two dots. Dots on paper must be positioned so that child must cross the mid-line with one hand.

    Yes, if child draws a continuous line crossing the mid-line of body.
    No, if child fails to join two dots, fails to cross mid-line.

4. Drawing circles with both hands   Yes   No   Comments

Examiner draws circles with both hands simultaneously at the blackboard. Child is asked to do the same.

Yes, if child can draw any kind of circle with both hands simultaneously.
No, if child is unable to use both hands simultaneously in drawing any kind of circle.

5. Cutting between two lines   Yes   No   Comments

Examiner takes piece of lined notebook paper and cuts between two lines. Child is then asked to cut between two lines as examiner did.

Yes, if child can cut between two lines.
No, if child cannot stay between two lines when cutting paper.

6. Touching fingers to thumb   Yes   No   Comments

Examiner touches thumb to each finger in succession. Child is asked to do the same.

Yes, if child can touch fingers and thumb on one hand in succession.
No, if child cannot touch a finger or fails to do so in succession.

C. Suggested Scoring Sheet

Fine Muscle Screening   Name _____

	Yes	No	Comments
1. Copying a square			
2. Buttoning			
3. Drawing of a line			
4. Drawing circles			
5. Cutting between lines			
6. Touching fingers to thumb			

Summary Comments:

Let Knowledge Grow
from More to More.
Author Unknown

Several publishing companies and various organizations were contacted in order to determine what evaluative techniques were available in perceptual-motor learning. In some cases, the actual test was reviewed, while in other instances, descriptive comments were taken from catalogs and brochures. The listing of testing devices is selective and in no way purports to be exhaustive.

Most companies request that orders for tests be placed on official stationery to insure that tests are being used by qualified educators. The descriptive information should help you in selecting an appropriate test.

Assessment Tools

Ayres Space Test by A. Jean Ayres is a performance test for children with visual perception difficulties.
This test measures spatial ability, position in space, and directionality. The test may be administered in 20-30 minutes, and normative data for 3-10 year olds is available. Complete test materials, manual, and twenty-five booklets are available from Western Psychological Services, Division of Manson Western Corporation, 12031 Wilshire Blvd., Los Angeles, Calif., 90025.

Engleman Basic Concept Inventory is a simple individual test given to children to determine their familiarity with basic concepts used in explanations and instructions.

Tests

Tests	Age Level	Year Developed	Available Forms	Data Available on Reliability & Validity	Available Norms (Test in normative data form)	Time for Administration	Special training needed to administer
Denver Developmental Screening Test	1 mo. 6 yr.	1967	1	yes	no	Variable	no
Denver Eye Screening Test	6 mo. &older	1972	1	no	no	few minutes	no
Engleman-Basic Concept Inventory	Preschool	1967	1	yes	yes	40-60 minutes	no
Memory-for-designs Test	8.5-60 yrs.	1946	1	yes	yes	10 min.	no
"Move-Grow-Learn"	Preschool-Primary	1971	1	no	no	variable	no
"Movement Skills Survey"	Preschool-3rd Grade	1971	1	no	no	2-25 min.	no
Oseretsky Tests of Motor Proficiency	4-16 yrs.	1946*	1	yes		20-30 min.	no
Robbins Speech Sound Discrimination and Verbal Imagery Type Tests	Preschool and Primary grades	1958	2	no	no	minimum 1 hour	no
Southern Calif. Sensory Integration Tests	4-10 yrs.	1972	1	yes	yes	1 hour	no
"The Developmental Test of Visual Motor Integration"	2-15 yrs	1967	2	yes	yes	15-20 min	no

*Currently being revised (late 73-early 74).

The test shows whether the child is familiar with conversational statements and whether he understands them. This inventory will provide the classroom teacher with information about the skills a child lacks.

If the classroom teacher administers this test, it will give insight to aid in remediation.

The "Basic Concept Inventory" of booklets, manuals, and picture cards may be purchased from Follett Publishing Company, 1010 W. Washington Boulevard, Chicago, Illinois 60607.

Evanston Early Identification Scale by Myrie Landsman and Harry Dillard is a device for identifying children who may have difficulty with school.

The test is valid for children five years to six years three months and may be administered to a group or an individual. 100 tests and teacher's manual are available from Follett Publishing Co. 1010 W. Washington Blvd., Chicago, Illinois 60607.

Goldman-Fristal-Woodcock Test of Auditory Discrimination is an individual test of ability to discriminate speech sounds in quiet and in noise.

It may be used on children four years and older and may be administered in 10-15 minutes. A pre-recorded tape provides standardized presentation. The subject first completes a training procedure to ensure he knows the word-picture associations before testing actually begins. The complete test kit (C-133) is available from American Guidance Services, Circle Pines, Minnesota 55014.

Kindergarten Auditory Screening Test by Jack Katz identifies children with auditory perceptual problems that may cause learning difficulties, especially in reading.

It tests three auditory perceptual skills: Discrimination of same and different word pairs; analysis and synthesis of words (sound blending); and figure-ground discrimination. The results from the tests offer guidelines for developmental training in auditory perception.

The record and teacher's manual and student response booklets can be purchased from Follett Publishing Co., 1010 W. Washington Blvd., Chicago, Ill. 60607.

Memory-For-Designs Test involves the presentation of simple geometric designs and the reproduction of these designs from immediate memory.

Much research has shown this test to be a very good detector of brain damage. With a poor performance, there is a high probability of brain disorder. It should be noted that the test shows relatively little correlation with either measures of intelligence or age. This test may be used as an effective differentiator of functional based brain disorder as opposed to those disorders associated with brain injury.

The complete tester's kit may be obtained from Psychological Test Specialists, Box 1441, Missoula, Montana 59801. Order must be accompanied by a statement as to the responsibility of the tester and the intended use of the test.

Movement Skills Survey by R.E. Arpet and T.F. Heutis is a check list to assist classroom teachers, physical education supervisors, school psychologists and other school personnel in evaluating selected aspects of a child's motor development.

It is intended for use with the Frostig-Maslow Move-Grow-Learn program and Movement Education: Theory and Practice. The child is observed in the classroom, playground or gymnasium in the following areas of sensory motor and movement skills: coordination and rhythm, agility, flexibility, strength, speed, balance, endurance and body awareness. This survey is available from Follett Publishing Co., Box 5705, Chicago, Illinois 60680.

Pre-Tests of Vision, Hearing, and Motor Coordination by Elizabeth L. Sullivan, Willis W. Clark and Ernest W. Tiegs are designed to screen for defects in vision, hearing, or motor coordination.

Levels vary from kindergarten to adult. 35 tests, manual and scoring key may be purchased from California Test Bureau, 2702 Monroe St., Madison, Wisconsin 53711.

Purdue Perceptual-Motor Survey by Eugene Roach and Newell C. Kephart offers perceptual-motor normative data for children first through fourth grade.

The materials in this book make it possible for the teacher to assess perceptual-motor problems in the classroom environment. This book may be ordered from Charles E. Merrill Publishing Co., 1300 Alum Creek Dr., Columbus, Ohio 43216.

Robbins Speech Sound Discrimination and Verbal Imagery Type Tests determine the types of speech sounds not differentiated by the child with a phonetic speech defect of a sensory origin.

These tests and exercises help him to see, hear, and feel the difference between the differing speech sounds in the given materials. The test booklet and scoring sheets for both younger and older children are available from Expression Co., 155 Columbus Ave., Boston, Mass. 02116

Southern California Sensory Integration Tests by A. Jean Ayres are a result of 10 years of research in the areas of perceptual and learning problems.

The tests measure visual, tactile, kinesthetic perception and several different types of motor performances. The entire battery of seventeen tests requires approximately one hour to administer and each test has been standardized on approximately 1,000 subjects with normative data given for ages 4-8. This series of tests includes space visualization, figure-ground perception, position in space, design copying, motor accuracy, kinesthesia, manual form perception, finger identification, graphesthesia, localization of tactile stimuli, double tactile stimuli perception, imitation of postures, crossing mid-line of body, bilateral motor coordination, right-left discrimination, standing balance with eyes open, and standing balance with eyes closed. Materials may be purchased from Western Psychological Services, Order Department, 12031 Wilshire Blvd., Los Angeles, California 90025.

The Denver Developmental Screening Test was developed by William K. Frankenburg, M.D., and Josiah B. Dobbs, Ph.D.

This test was devised to screen for evidence of slow or delayed development in infants and preschool children. The test covers four areas of development: fine motor, language, fine motor adaptive and personal-social.

Test Kits, manuals, and forms may be purchased from the LADOCA Project and Publishing Foundation, Inc., East 51st Avenue and Lincoln Street, Denver, Colorado 80216.

The Developmental Test of Visual-Motor Integration by Keith E. Beeriz measures the degree to which perception and motor behavior are integrated in young children.

This test contains either 15 (short form) or 24 (long form) geometric forms for the child to reproduce. The forms are arranged in order of increasing difficulty. This test will help the classroom teacher in the screening of perceptual motor development by reflecting problems in visual perception, hand control and coordination between the two suggested teaching techniques and other materials for use by the student are included in the manual. The short form or long form, scoring manual, stimulus cards and assessment work sheets are available from Follett Publishing Company, Box 5705, Chicago, Illinois 60680.

The Oseretsky Motor Proficiency Test was translated by Maria Irene Leite da Casta

This test measures fine and gross motor development of children and may be compared in structure to the Binet-Simon scale for measuring intelligence. The test has six component parts: general static coordination, dynamic coordination of the hands, general dynamic coordination, motor speed, simultaneous voluntary movements and synkinesia (performance without superfluous movements).

Test equipment, including manual and 25 record blanks is available from the American Guidance Service, Inc., Circle Pines, Minnesota 55014.

Valett Developmental Survey of Basic Training Abilities by Robert E. Valett may be used to evaluate the developmental status of children from age two to seven. The survey covers the areas of motor integration and physical development, tactile discrimination, language discrimination, auditory discrimination, language development and verbal fluency and conceptual development. The teacher may use the results to determine if additional evaluation is needed or to help in planning the educational activities. The manual, workbook and scoring booklet may be purchased from Consulting Psychologists Press, 577 College Avenue, Palo Alto, Ca. 94306.

PART III
Designing an Action Program

CHAPTER ONE

A Team Approach

And he who has deserved to drink from the ocean of life deserves to fill his cup from your little stream.

                                                                Kahlil Gibran

Often times it is a teacher who first recognizes, or at least is willing to admit, that the Marys, Johnnys, Billys, and Mikes of whom we spoke earlier in this book do indeed have serious problems. Problems that can and do affect their family life, their social adjustment, their academic achievement, and their success in physical or sports endeavors. Frequently, it is failure or poor behavior in school that finally causes the parents to seek professional help. Sometimes the help comes too late, sometimes not at all. Elementary school teachers are in a unique position to detect these problems early enough in a child's school life that help can be started and a program of specific remedial activities begun.

If Mary is in a physical education class and her teacher notes extremely poor hand-eye coordination, balance, spatial awareness, or any other of a number of perceptual-motor problems, that should be enough to alert the teacher to the possibility that other difficulties may exist. Using the team approach method, the next step should be to contact Mary's classroom teacher to see how she is functioning in academic tasks—and so it begins, one interested person, then two, then three, and finally a whole team of interested people trying to help one little child before the wrong patterns and habits are ingrained so deeply that they often become irreversible or irreparable.

Who is on this team? Logically, the first important members are those who work directly with the child—the parents, the classroom teacher, the physical education teacher, and the guidance counselor. Next, the medical doctor or pediatrician, and others are consulted as the needs of the child are determined—possibly a child psychiatrist, a county health nurse, a speech therapist, a teacher of the emotionally disturbed, or a vision specialist. Most of the team members or consultants are available through normal school channels.

When a series of perceptual-motor difficulties are detected in a child, there may be a multitude of other problems present thus making the team approach method of problem solving not only desirable but also necessary. Children with perceptual-motor impairments may also demonstrate many of the following traits:

1. Hyperactivity
2. Emotional instability
3. Short attention spans and distractibility
4. Impulsivity
5. Short memories and thinking disorders
6. Specific learning disabilities in arithmetic, writing, spelling, and/or reading.
7. Speech and hearing disorders

The team approach method examines the whole child and attempts to find appropriate solutions to as many of his difficulties as possible. The earlier that the problems are diagnosed and treated the greater the chance of marked improvement, and the greater the chance of academic, social, and/or physical or motor success.

A sensitive, effective teacher is one who knows her children well—not just their names and faces, but their needs, desires, wants, strengths, and weaknesses, and then uses that knowledge to detect learning problems which may have a solution if they are recognized and treated early in the child's school life.

The rest of this chapter is devoted to presenting a detailed case study of a child from an elementary school. In this particular school there were many specialists available to aid in the administration of the program developed for a child named Jimmy. This study could serve as a model to show how a team approach method can function effectively in a school environment. It should be stressed, however, that this was a rather unique situation and many schools do not have as many specialists as this one had. The average school, for example, might not have a perceptual-motor specialist, but in most cases the physical education teacher and the classroom teacher working together can accomplish the same things. The language specialist described below was concerned mainly with language development, whereas many language specialists in the elementary schools today are concerned with speech defects. Again, the classroom teacher with a little extra planning can reinforce the areas of weakness in the normal classroom setting—sometimes on an individual basis, sometimes in a small group, sometimes by the use of an aide (paid by the school), a parent helper, or by using an advanced upper-grade child for special tutoring.

Once the problems have been detected, the teacher should begin a remedial program as soon as possible. With a little extra planning, a lot of imagination, and the help of others interested in the child, progress can be made—even if the only ones available to help are the classroon teacher, the physical education teacher, and the guidance counselor.

Jimmy

The Problem

Jimmy's mother was worried. She was getting him ready for his first day at kindergarten. It should have been a big day in their lives, but instead of it being a joyful, happy occasion it was strangely sad and quiet. His mother had been worried about him since the day he was born for his was by far the most difficult of her four deliveries—long, painful hours spent in labor and finally a breech delivery. In the years that followed, Jimmy appeared to be a normal, healthy youngster, and yet his growth and development over the years had been very different from that of his brothers and sisters. He was slower in learning to walk, in talking, and in accomplishing other motor tasks appropriate for his age. His mother convinced herself that these differences were probably due to a slower maturation rate, after all he was the baby of the family, and that it was unfair to compare him to the other children. She had discussed these things with her husband, but he said she was being silly and that Jimmy was just taking a little longer to develop than the others had. Besides, he reasoned, the doctor would have told them if anything was wrong. And so the years passed. Now Jimmy was five years old and was going to school for the first time, but deep inside his mother knew he was not ready for school. She knew he did not have the basic skills that the other children had when they entered school. He did not know how to tie his shoes, he did not know his right hand from his left, he confused the names of colors, he could not count to 10, he did not know the alphabet. Why? She had worked with him, helped him, but for some reason he had not responded, and often the ''learning sessions'' were wrought with anger and frustration—she wound up yelling and he wound up crying. What had she done wrong? Why was Jimmy different? In looking for answers to those questions, she had feelings of guilt. It must have been her fault, she reasoned. Maybe she had not been patient enough; maybe she had not devoted enough time to him. She was not working when the other children were small, but with Jimmy it was different. She had to work to help supplement the family income, so she had gotten a job when he was six months old. Whether or not she admitted it, she had convinced herself that it was her fault that Jimmy was not ready for kindergarten.

On that first school day Jimmy's mother held him tightly in her arms hoping she was wrong and that everything would be alright. She watched him walk out of the front door and down the street with a lump in her throat and a prayer on her lips.

In school, Jimmy was lost from the very first day. He was thrown into a world of pictures, numbers, letters, colors, and concepts which he could not understand. He was given crayons that broke in his hand when he tried to draw or color, scissors that he could not make cut, questions that he could not answer, balls that he could not throw or catch. He was confused, frustrated, and angry, and most of all he hated school.

The Approach

It did not take Jimmy's teacher long to realize that he had some serious problems. He had difficulty manipulating crayons and scissors; his large muscle movements were awkward causing him to bump into chairs and tables that the other children moved around and between with relative ease; he had tremendous difficulty reproducing even the simplest lines or numbers; colors and concepts such as right and left were presented to him, practiced with him, and almost immediately forgotten by him; his eye-hand coordination was poor; he had an extremely short attention span; and he did not get along well with his classmates.

His teacher decided that she needed more information about him before she could decide what action should be taken. She referred him to the school guidance counselor for testing. He was administered the Slosoon Intelligence Test which showed his I.Q. to be within the low-normal range. On the basis of that test, he was referred to psychological services for further psychometric testing. The Weschler Intelligence Scale for Children (WISC) was administered and it showed a wide difference between his verbal and performance abilities indicating that Jimmy did indeed have a problem. After reviewing the results of the tests, the teacher and counselor decided that his parents should come in for a conference.

The conference was held with the parents, the teacher, the counselor, the physical education teacher, the language specialist, and the perceptual-motor specialist. After discussing the problems Jimmy was having in school, his mother realized that they were basically the same "seemingly insignificant" little things that she had noticed since his birth—he just had not accomplished the things that a child his age and of his family background should have accomplished. It was decided at the conference that Jimmy should be taken to the family doctor and given a thorough physical examination to evaluate his current physical status and to search for possible systemic disease. This time the difficulties that his teachers and mother had noticed would be explained in detail to the doctor before the examination, along with the results obtained from the psychometric testing. A second conference was scheduled for a later date to discuss the results of the doctor's examination and to decide where to go from there. Jimmy's parents left the conference with mixed emotions, but they were determined to find out what was wrong, and how and why it had happened. The problems that had been so easily explained away for so many years were now to be examined in detail.

At the second conference the parents reported on the doctor's examination and diagnosis. They told with some difficulty, how the doctor diagnosed Jimmy's problem as minimal brain dysfunction possibly caused by his traumatic birth. He had reached this diagnosis by pooling the findings of the medical examination, the family history of the child, the scores of the WISC, and the observations made by his parents and teachers. It took some time for the parents to accept this diagnosis and to sort out their feelings and emotions, but the most important thing was to help Jimmy and they were willing to do anything they could to help.

The Treatment

Diagnosing that Jimmy had a minimal brain dysfunction was only the beginning. A coordinated program with the involvement of parents, teachers, and the physician was begun.

The perceptual-motor specialist administered the Jean Ayre's Southern California Perceptual-Motor Test and found Jimmy to be well below the standard score for his age group in all six of the tests: standing balance eyes open; standing balance eyes closed; imitation of postures; crossing the mid-line of the body; bilateral motor coordination; and right and left discrimination. A program of large muscle activities was designed by the perceptual-motor specialist and the physical education teacher to improve the areas of difficulty. Many of the activities chosen are listed in the playground activities section of this book. Included in the program were such features as:

1. The improvement of basic body movements, inherent locomotor and non-locomotor skill, and utilization of symmetrical and asymmetrical activities to strengthen concepts of laterality and bilaterality.
2. The enhancement of the child's perception of body image, the relationship of the body to surrounding space, and the awareness of direction.
3. The development of a sense of dynamic and static balance.
4. The development of specific coordinated movements including eye-hand, eye-foot.
5. The development of manipulative skills (balls, hoops, ropes, wands).
6. The enhancement of the child's natural rhythmic patterns.

These large muscle activities were practiced in the physical education classes and were also practiced at home. A student helper from the fifth grade worked with Jimmy on the days when he did not have physical education.

The parents started a program of perceptual-motor activities at home using the book "Daily Sensorimotor Training Activities" by Braley, Konicki, and Leedy, as a guide for ideas and activities. The older children in the family enjoyed the activities in the book and frequently worked with Jimmy on their own.

The language specialist saw Jimmy three times a week. She administered the Boehm Test of Basic Concepts, and found that his raw score placed him in the 40th percentile. The SRA Language I Kit was the primary curriculum material used in the class sessions. This instructional system utilized a direct teaching approach which focuses on the language of instruction: polar opposites, prepositions, pronouns, action statements, categories, plurals, and the difference between "guessing" and "knowing."

The perceptual-motor specialist saw Jimmy two times a week and used the Fairbanks-Robinson Program for Perceptual-Motor Development, Levels 1 and 2. This program is designed to aid in the development of those perceptual-motor abilities believed to be prerequisite to academic functioning. It includes line exercises, line and form reproduction, discrimination and recognition of basic shapes, coloring and cutting exercises, figure-ground discrimination, spatial concepts and spatial relationships.

The school guidance counselor worked with Jimmy several times a week in a small group setting. The emphasis was improving self-concept and learning how to get along with other children. Characteristics of such a counseling relationship included use of many of the following: verbal exploration of situations and emotions, expression of feelings through drawing and painting, and by using self-concept workbooks.

The Thomas Self-Concept Values Test[1] was administered to Jimmy by the counselor. It reflected a lowered self-concept and negative values held in areas of size (physique) and sharing with peers.

The classroom teacher worked to reinforce all areas of learning for Jimmy. Aware of his problems, interest centers were set up for him and other children with similar difficulties, around the room. She also made up a special packet of activities for him which focused on his special areas of weakness: concepts of size and directions, colors, numbers, shapes, letters, coloring, cutting, and others. She helped him on an individual basis when possible, in small groups, and had many activities which he could work on by himself or with an aide. She also made special arrangements for one of the advanced fifth grade girls to come work with him for 30 minutes each day. A special folder with daily activities was organized for this purpose.

The family doctor was kept informed of Jimmy's progress and was available for consultation when needed. He was in a unique position of familiarity and trust with the child and his family.

This remedial program continued for a period of seven months from November 1972 to May 1973. The pretests were administered in October and the posttests during the last two weeks in May.

The Results

Southern California Perceptual-Motor Test—Jimmy showed significant differences in five of the six tests administered: imitation of postures, crossing the mid-line of the body, bilateral motor coordination, right-left discrimination, standing balance eyes open. Improvement was noted, but it was not significant in the standing balance with the eyes closed.

Boehm Test of Basic Concepts—Jimmy improved from a 40th percentile score on the pretest to an 80th percentile score on the posttest.

Thomas Self-Concept Values Test—Jimmy improved 20 Standard Score points above his pretest indicating significant progress and development.

Neither the Slosson nor the WISC were repeated at the end of the year.

Jimmy's improvement in academic, social and motor functions was observed by all of the teachers working with him. He began to like school, he seemed content and happy, and he got along well with his classmates. His ability to write, draw, color, and cut improved significantly. His large muscle movements were more smoothly coordinated and he seemed to move with more assurance and self-confidence. All in all he improved and progressed in all areas. Some of the improvement was no doubt due to normal maturation, some to added attention that he received from his teachers, and some to the team approach method of looking at and working with the whole child. Through the team effort teachings were reinforced by two or three people, as were Jimmy's feelings of personal worth and value.

A detailed report of the program conducted throughout the year was placed in Jimmy's confidential cumulative folder at school. Suggestions were also included for his next teacher in hopes that his individual needs would continue to be met. He still had much to learn, and no one was sure how far he would be able to go, but definite progress had been made and with help from his teachers and parents would continue to be made.

Summary

Research has tended to prove, as shown earlier in this book, that not all children improve in academic areas when placed in a program of perceptual-motor development. In the case study presented here, several areas were being emphasized at the same time: perceptual-motor, language development and guidance and counseling. It would be impossible to determine which of these areas had the most OR least effect on Jimmy's improvement. It would seem that they all made important contributions.

If through a program of large muscle developmental activities a child learns to move and manage his body with confidence and ease then he should be able to function more efficiently in terms of movement for the rest of his life. That contribution alone would seem to make a large muscle perceptual-motor program worthwhile.

As the child with perceptual-motor problems grows older, research has tended to prove that remedial activities should be more specific to the academic tasks required in the classroom—fine motor tasks related to improving the child's ability to read, write, think and work with numbers.

It would appear then, that a combination of large muscle and fine motor developmental activities could help a child with perceptual-motor impairments both inside and outside the classroom.

---

[1]Thomas Self-Concept Values Test available from Combined Motivation Educational Systems, Inc., 6300 River Road, Rosemont, IL 60018

CHAPTER TWO

Developmental Activities

. . . all experience is an arch wherethro' gleams that untraveled world, whose margin fades forever and forever when I move.

Author Unknown

Brief Overview

Previous chapters have discussed the basic meaning and significance of perceptual-motor development in the young child. This included an overview of various learning theories from which the perceptual-motor concept was developed, and a summarization of perceptual-motor learning research. The available diagnostic tools which were presented will help the teacher to assess the child's perceptual-motor skills which are necessary for the optimum development of his physical and academic potentials.

It is significant to remember that perceptual abilities are an outgrowth of past learning experiences and neurological maturation. Upon entering school these abilities are generally developed in each child to some degree. Keep in mind, however, that varying maturation rates and/or lack of meaningful early childhood experiences can make a perceptual-motor program quite necessary for many primary aged youngsters. Such a program then should be designed to improve those necessary perceptual abilities considered as prerequisites to optimal academic functioning. Every child, of course, should have the opportunity to develop those perceptual skills considered necessary for academic success and movement efficiency.

Children lacking perceptual motor abilities may well be discovered when the teacher administers a diagnostic screening test. Where improvement is necessary, perceptual-motor activities can be conducted in accordance with the child's specific needs.

Activities

The purpose of this chapter is to provide you with a variety of exciting activities and games designed to help children develop and reinforce their perceptual abilities. For purposes of clarity and selection the activities and games are divided into two main categories; classroom activities and playground activities. The classroom activities relate more specifically to academic skills and can be incorporated into the classroom teacher's curriculum. Major headings include:

1. Pre-Reading
2. Reading
3. Pre-Writing
4. Writing
5. Mathematics
6. Spelling

The playground activities are chiefly concerned with the large muscle development of the child and would most likely be included in the physical education program. Activity areas are:

1. Balance
2. Space and Direction
3. Coordination
   a. Eye-hand
   b. Eye-foot
   c. Symmetrical
4. Body Image
5. Rhythms

It should be noted that many of these games and activities are appropriate for both the classroom and playground and can therefore be used interchangeably by the classroom teacher and the physical education specialist.

Guidelines to Activity

"Watch me Miss Roberts . . . look Mr. Smith I can do it!" These words and others like them have been echoed by thousands of school children on playgrounds across the country. It signals a feeling of happiness through achievement which fosters self-satisfaction and recognition—key elements to future learning success. All too often, however, the voices of children are silenced by the frustrations that accompany repeated failure with tasks which may be far beyond their ability for a variety of reasons.

It is essential that the teacher choose activities that are commensurate with the child's developmental level. Although the activities included here are designed primarily for children from pre-school age through second grade, they may be used for any child functioning below age expectancy in basic perceptual-motor skills. For example, assume that a child has great difficulty in walking a balance board when his peers, who are of the same age, can do so with relative ease. A screening test for balance further confirms this difficulty. It would be appropriate to start at the child's level and seek to have him progress from simple to more complex balance skills. Perhaps a good starting point would be to have the child walk forward and backward on a painted line on the floor. After the child is skillful at this he may wish to walk on a length of board 4'' wide which is lying on the ground. In effect, you are taking "cues" from the child and presenting progressive learning tasks in relation to his changing needs. By presenting the child with a variety of interesting balancing skills within his developmental reach, successful achievement with all its ramifications may be realized.

A valuable teaching method called movement exploration may also be used in presenting many of these activities to your children. This approach enables the teacher to use guiding questions to help the child realize an obtainable goal. To illustrate, assume the objective is to help a child understand various bases of support he is capable of making with his body. The teacher might say, "support yourself on the floor using any three body parts." "Find a new way using three body parts." "Can you use four body parts; two parts?" By using a little imagination the teacher can structure many opportunities for the child to create a variety of supports. Subsequent teacher reinforcement can make this a most valuable learning experience for the child.

The benefits of using a movement exploration approach with these activities is found in the non-competitive atmosphere. This permits each child to work on an individual skill level which may be quite different from the next child's. In this fashion a meaningful individual level of accomplishment can be set by teacher and child, rather than one group standard which may not be realistic for some children. In effect then, the teacher is not "building in" potential failure but success. Thus by using the movement exploration approach, not only will the child find his own level of achievement but, all children are assured success.

Remember that through a well-planned program of meaningful perceptual-motor activities a child can be guided to the optimal development of his perceptual abilities. Although more research needs to be conducted, available evidence tends to indicate that the children mentioned in Chapter I can benefit greatly from a program of developmental perceptual-motor activities.

One final word about the use of these activities. Emphasis thus far has been given to helping those children who exhibit deficiencies in perceptual-motor ability and how you can help them. Also, keep in mind however, these activities may be used with children who do not display perceptual-motor deficiencies. They may be used to help them reinforce, in new and exciting ways, the channels through which they learn. How exciting it would be for a normally achieving child to put his hand in a "mystery" box in which he could not see what was inside but rather had to rely on his sense of touch to identify it! Thus, touch and past experience would be combined to identify the object which would serve as an excellent reinforcement for touch perception.

The activities presented here will hopefully be useful in helping the teacher plan a challenging and meaningful developmental program for children. However, these activities represent only a few of the varied and stimulating activities available for use.

Classroom Activities

Pre-Reading Skills

The activities in this section can be used to provide children with much-needed practice in moving from left to right, downward, and across the page in new and challenging ways. This type of reinforcement may provide the child with the basic skills needed for successful reading. Such learning cues as, "start at the left side of your page and go to the right," "follow the line of print across the page," "move from line to line down the page," etc. must all be mastered and understood.

ACTIVITY: Line Tracing

EQUIPMENT: Large sheet of paper with four lines, one inch wide, drawn vertically down the page. An "X" should be drawn at the top of each line on the page.

EXPLANATION:

1. Give each child a sheet of paper with the one-inch wide lines drawn in.

2. Have the child place his finger on the "X" at the top of the first line. "Can you move your finger all the way down the line to the bottom of the page?" "Now put your finger on the "X" at the top of the next line and move your finger all the way down to the bottom of the page."

3. Have the child continue without stopping until he has completed all lines.

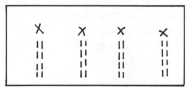

HINTS:

1. Young children may need help in locating the "X" at the top of each line.

2. When the child has mastered tracing with his finger, the page may be placed under a clear sheet of plastic and a

large crayon may be used to trace down the center of each line.

3. The other lines illustrated should be practiced in the same manner.

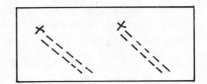

Reading

Activities in the area of reading provide children with the opportunity to correctly identify words through games involving movement. Reading skills such as word recognition and understanding the real meaning of words can be greatly enhanced through these games. Specific areas of reading comprehension include identification of words, arranging words in sequential order in sentences, matching abstraction (words) with concrete representation (pictures), matching alike words, recognizing body parts and demonstrating what function they perform, and finally acting out the meaning of a printed sentence.

ACTIVITY: Find the Animal

EQUIPMENT: Word and matching picture cards of different animals. A picture card and identifying word card will be needed for each child.

EXPLANATION:

1. Children are divided into two or more teams. Each child is given a picture of an animal. Teams should be seated and numbered one, two, three, etc. so each child will know when his turn comes.

2. The word cards, for the animals are in a pile 15' to 20' away.

3. "Look at the picture you are holding; when I say go, the first person on each team will go to the pile of word cards and try to find the name of the animal in the picture. If you are holding the picture of a monkey then you find the card that says MONKEY. After you have found the card, bring it back to your

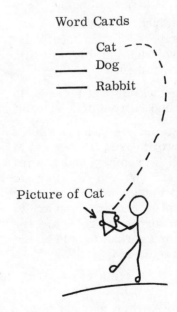

Word Cards

_____ Cat
_____ Dog
_____ Rabbit

Picture of Cat

team and tag the next person. Keep going until everyone in the group has the name of his animal."

HINTS:

1. Children should go to the card pile moving like the animal in their picture.

2. Other things may be substituted for animals, such as: modes of transportation, fruits, colors, etc.

3. The picture cards may be made by cutting pictures from discarded magazines.

ACTIVITY: Run for the Word

EQUIPMENT: Stack of word cards for each group. Numbered cards (1-2-3 . . .) for each group.

EXPLANATION:

1. Divide your children into two or more teams. The children in each group are numbered consecutively. Give each child a card with his number.

2. A stack of word cards is placed in front of each team.

3. "Across the room is a stack of word cards. I am going to call a number and a word which you can find in your word stack. When I call your number and word you are to run across the room and try to be the first to hold up the correct card."

HINTS:

1. The teacher may use a picture card instead of calling the word.

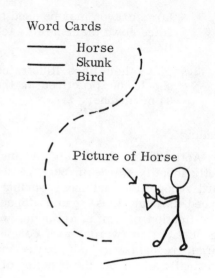

Word Cards

——— Horse
——— Skunk
——— Bird

Picture of Horse

Word Cards

——Hat
——Coat
——Dog
——Pencil

Word Cards

——Hat
——Coat
——Dog
——Pencil

"Number three coat!"

2. Ask children to hop, skip, go on hands and knees, etc., to the stack of word cards.

ACTIVITY: Matching Words

EQUIPMENT: Two sets of matching word cards such as:

Red cards	Blue cards
eye	see
ear	hear
tongue	talk
hand	write
feet	walk

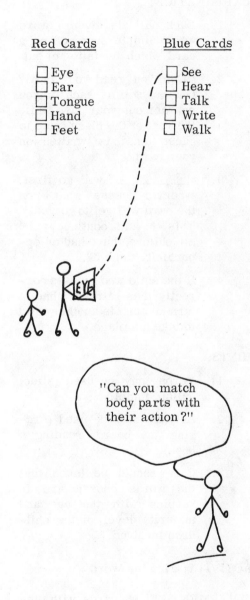

EXPLANATION:

1. Class is divided into two or more groups.

2. "I want to see if you can match some of your body parts with an action they perform. What do your eyes do?" . . . "That's right; they see." "What about your ears; what do they do?" . . . "That's right; they hear."

3. Each group is given two sets of cards. "Can you take each red card and find a blue card which matches it."

HINTS:

1. The matching word cards may be sound-alikes such as:
   deer-dear
   pear-pair
   sew-so

2. The matching word cards may be opposites.

3. This activity may be used as a relay race.

ACTIVITY: Read and Do

EQUIPMENT: Word or sentence cards.

EXPLANATION:

1. Each child is given a word or a simple sentence on a card which he is to act out.

2. "Can you read your card? One at a time each of you can act out your card while the rest of the class tries to guess what is written on your card."

3. "_____ will go first. Whoever guesses what is on the card will get to go next." This should continue until all children have had an opportunity to be IT.

4. If the child who guesses correctly has already had a turn he selects another child to take his place.

HINTS:

1. Verbs may be used (slide, gallop, jump).

2. Actions may be used (erasing the board, reading a book).

3. Care should be taken that the words chosen are in keeping with the age and maturity level of the children involved.

(The same child)

ACTIVITY: Find the Word

EQUIPMENT: Flash cards with pictures or familiar objects such as animals, colors, toys, etc. A matching word grid should be drawn on the floor, in the sand or painted on canvas.

EXPLANATION:

1. Children may work individually taking turns or in groups.

2. If children work in groups they should be numbered one, two, three, etc., so each will know when his turn is.

3. If working in groups a separate grid may be used for each child or a very large grid (each word three feet square) may be used simultaneously for four or five groups.

4. "When I flash a picture run to the grid and stand on the word which matches the picture I am holding. The first person to stand on the correct word wins a point for their team. After the winner is called, go to the back of the line and wait for your next turn."

5. This should continue until each child has had several turns. The team with the most points wins the game.

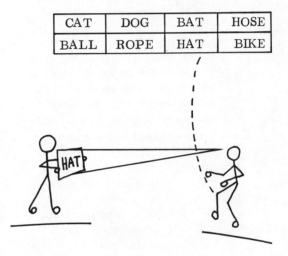

CAT	DOG	BAT	HOSE
BALL	ROPE	HAT	BIKE

HINTS:

1. Scoring may be varied to give a point for all correct responses regardless of who reaches the grid first. This type of scoring would be most appropriate when an individual grid is provided for each group.

2. For variation the printed word may be flashed and the child can run to the picture on a grid.

ACTIVITY: Make a Sentence

EQUIPMENT: Stacks of word cards for each child or group of children. Each stack should make a simple sentence when put together.

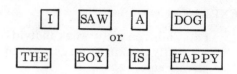

EXPLANATION:

1. Divide the children into groups of 3-4 and have them sit on the floor.

2. "The name of this game is Make A Sentence. Listen very carefully while I explain how we play. Across the room in front of each group is a stack of word cards. There is one word on each card. When the words are put together they make a sentence like: I saw a dog or The boy is happy. When I say "Go" the first person in each group will run across the room, pick up one card, bring it back to his group and then sit down. Keep going until all of the cards are picked up. The first group to make the correct sentence with the cards wins the game. Make the sentence on the floor in front of you."

HINTS:

1. The sentences should be kept very simple.

2. Children may be asked to run, skip, hop, etc. to pick up the cards.

3. This activity may be adapted to smaller numbers of children by putting one child to each stack of cards.

Pre-writing skills

Through pre-writing activities children are encouraged to exercise their fine muscle coordination through such activities as coloring and cutting with a pair of scissors. It is, of course, extremely important that a child be able to master his ability to handle those instruments in a rather general way before we can legitimately expect him to handle a pencil with enough dexterity to shape individual letters and symbols.

ACTIVITY: Cutting

EQUIPMENT: Scissors with large bottom loop, and paper.

EXPLANATION:

1. Give each child a pair of scissors.

2. Help the child hold the scissors in the following manner: the thumb is placed in the top finger loop and the middle and ring fingers in the larger bottom loop. The index finger is used to guide and control the scissors. The child should practice cutting plain paper until he establishes the appropriate cutting action. Each cutting movement is stopped before the blades are completely closed. This allows for smooth cutting and prevents tearing of the paper.

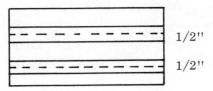

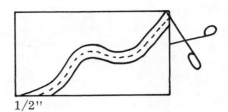

HINTS:

1. Watch the child closely as he cuts, guiding him with verbal cues.

2. He will need cues in opening the scissors and sliding them forward.

3. The scissors should be held in the dominant hand.

4. Once a smooth and controlled cutting action has been established provide the child with other cutting experiences, such as:

    —cutting down the center of 1/2" lines drawn across a piece of paper without cutting the edges of the lines. For curved lines the paper should be held and turned in the non-dominant hand.

    —figures (animals, shapes, objects) can be cut out.

Writing

You may repeat any of the following activities for letter recognition simply by combining large and small letters, and upper and lower case letters. You can expect the child to respond, for the most part, using an upper case letter. This added recognition makes the activity a little more difficult and should be done only after the child is familiar with the various ways to write the same letter.

ACTIVITY: Letter Shapes

EQUIPMENT: Chalkboard and open floor space or sand.

EXPLANATION:

1. Have children sit down on the floor or in the sand on the playground.

2. "I am going to write a letter on the chalkboard. I want you to write the letter in the sand."

HINTS:

1. After the child has had some practice making the letters from visual cues, verbal cues may be substituted (say the letter and have the child make it).

ACTIVITY: Walk Out The Letter

EQUIPMENT: Sandbox on floor and chalkboard.

EXPLANATION:

1. Children are standing in an open space in the classroom, in a large sandbox or on the playground.

2. "I am going to write a letter on the chalkboard and I want you to walk out the letter on the floor."

HINTS:

1. Other methods of movement may be used: forward, backward, sideways, heel to toe, hopping, etc.

2. If it is more convenient for the teacher, flash cards with letters may be used rather than the chalkboard.

ACTIVITY: Hear, See and Find the Letter

EQUIPMENT: Chalkboard and letter grid on the floor.

EXPLANATION:

1. Children are divided into two or more groups with five or six children in a group.

2. "Across the room from each of your groups is a letter grid. I am going to call out a letter and write it on the board. The first person in each group will run across the room and stand on the correct letter."

3. Unless the teacher gives both verbal and visual cues the child should not respond.

HINTS:

1. This activity encourages the child to look and listen.

2. Variation: Once this activity has been practiced sufficiently, the verbal cue may be eliminated. The child would then respond only to the visual cue on the chalkboard, vice versa.

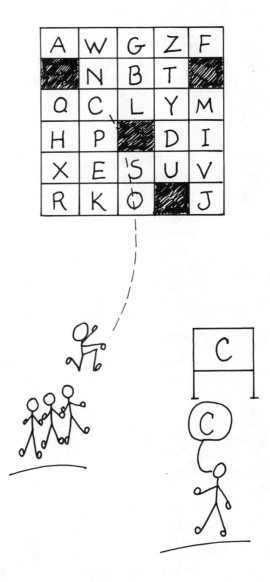

Mathematics

Mathematics activities need not be dull and uninteresting. The following activities are designed to give children the chance to feel, see, hear, and become numbers, symbols, shapes, and concepts. The focus of these skills improvement games is to involve children in a fun and exciting way in the learning of mathematics.

ACTIVITY: Dot-to-Dot Shapes

EQUIPMENT: Chalkboard and chalk.

EXPLANATION:

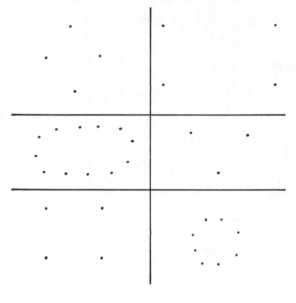

1. Dots are placed on the chalkboard to represent the different shapes.

2. "The dots on the chalkboard may be connected to form different shapes. Can you connect the lines very carefully? Step back. What shape have you drawn?"

3. Each child should have an opportunity to draw each shape.

HINTS:

1. The dots may be drawn on paper and connected by using a large crayon.

ACTIVITY: Recognition and Discrimination of Shapes

EQUIPMENT: A sheet of white construction paper for each of the six basic shapes (○ □ △ ▭ ◯ ◇). The shape is drawn on the paper about 1" wide.

EXPLANATION:

1. Children are divided into groups of six. Each group is provided with a set of the basic shapes, and each child is given one of the shapes.

2. "With your index finger trace around the shape staying within the lines and trying not to touch the sides."

3. The shapes are rotated within the group until each child has traced every shape.

HINTS:

1. The characteristics of each shape should be discussed before tracing.

2. After finger tracing, a small sheet of clear plastic may be placed over the drawing to protect it, and a large crayon may be substituted for the index finger. The crayon may be erased with a tissue.

3. Have the child look around the room, in magazines, etc. to identify and name the shapes he finds.

ACTIVITY: Walk the Shape

EQUIPMENT: Various geometric shapes drawn on the floor using chalk or tape. Chalkboard.

EXPLANATION:

1. Divide your children into groups of three or more.

2. "Watch me while I draw a shape on the board. Then one of you in each group will find the same shape on the floor and walk on that shape."

HINTS:

1. Be sure each child has a chance to walk on all the shapes.

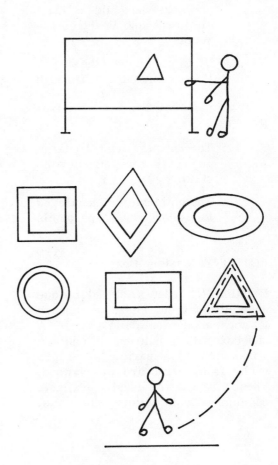

2. The child can skip, hop, tiptoe, heel to toe, etc. around the shape.

3. Ask the child to find a new way to move around the shape.

ACTIVITY: Explore the Shapes

EQUIPMENT: Various shapes placed around the room to enable the child to go under, over, around, through, and between them. These shapes may be cut from cardboard, plywood or plastic pipe. Smaller shapes are also needed as examples.

EXPLANATION:

1. Teacher holds up a shape and asks the child to find a similar shape in the classroom.

2. "Can you go over the shape? Under? Around? Through it?"

HINTS:

1. The shapes must be large and easily recognized by the child.

2. The child may be encouraged to explore the shape on his own.

ACTIVITY: Mystery Box

EQUIPMENT: Get a closed opaque container with a hole large enough to accommodate a child's hand. A shoebox with a hole cut in one end works nicely. A variety of shapes made from cardboard or plywood. These shapes are usually available commercially in building block sets.

EXPLANATION:

1. ''Close your eyes while I put one shape into the mystery box. Then open your eyes and put your hand into the mystery box and tell me what shape you feel.''

HINTS:

1. Three dimensional shapes are much easier to identify and are recommended.

ACTIVITY: Do You See It?

EQUIPMENT: Various three dimensional shapes available commercially or made from cardboard (ex., square, triangle).

EXPLANATION:

1. Make a variety of shapes that correspond with objects you have in the classroom.

2. ''When I give you a shape see if you can find a similar shape anywhere in the room. Daniel, can you find a shape like this?''

HINT:

1. Place shapes around the room and have the child try to find them and match them with similar shapes in the room.

ACTIVITY: Build the Shape

EQUIPMENT: Building blocks, cubes, books or any objects which can be stacked or placed end on end.

Classroom Setting

Table

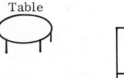

Chalkboard

Globe of World

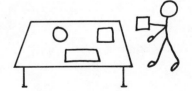

EXPLANATION:

1. Teacher calls a shape and the child builds it.

2. "Can you build a rectangle?"

HINTS:

1. May be individual or group effort.

2. Each group may be given a different shape.

3. Fancy materials are not necessary. Scrap lumber, empty containers from kitchen, etc. may be used successfully.

ACTIVITY: What Am I?

EQUIPMENT: None

EXPLANATION:

1. The children can work in groups of two, three or four.

2. "Each group (2, 3, or 4) get together and think of a number you can be together. The rest of us will then try to guess what number you have made."

HINTS:

1. Some numbers may be made by one child acting alone.

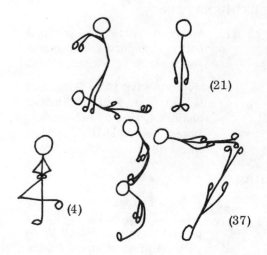

ACTIVITY: Move to the Number

EQUIPMENT: A grid painted on the floor. The grid can also be made on a surface such as oil cloth, canvas, etc. It should be sturdy and made with a non-slip backing so it will not slide on the floor.

EXPLANATION:

1. "When I call a number or sign see if you can find it on the grid and stand on it."

HINTS:

1. You can have the child move to the numbers and signs in different ways such as hopping, skipping, etc.

ACTIVITY: Matching Numbers

EQUIPMENT: Two sets of numbered squares for each group of 10 children.

EXPLANATION:

1. Class is divided into groups of ten. Each group is provided with a grid made from one of the sets of numbers. The other group of ten numbers is located 15 to 20 feet away.

2. "On the signal 'go' the first child in each group will run across the room and pick up any number, return and place it over the same number on your grid."

3. This will continue until the entire grid is covered.

HINTS:

1. Teams may be increased or decreased by adding or subtracting numbers.

2. For variation children may be asked to hop, skip or gallop across the floor.

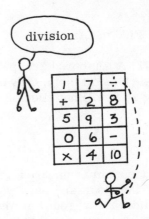

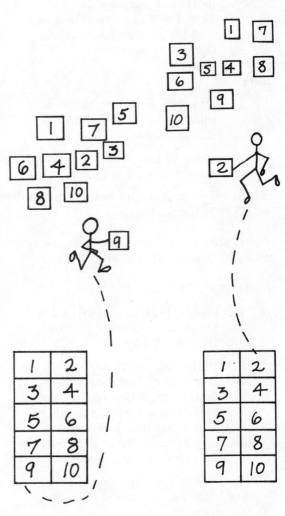

ACTIVITY: Find the Answer

EQUIPMENT: A numbered grid painted on the floor. The grid can also be made on a surface such as oil cloth, canvas, etc. It should be sturdy and made with a non-slip backing so it will not slide on the floor.

Chalkboard.

EXPLANATION:

1. Place your numbered grid on the floor and have your children sit around it while you explain the game to them.

2. "I will write a problem on the board such as 2 + 2 = ? Then I will ask one of you to look for, run and stand on the correct answer."

HINTS:

1. You can also use division, subtraction and multiplication problems.

2. Older children may be given problems which require two grids for the answer (Ex., 9 x 9 = 81).

3. Ask the child to respond using different body parts.

ACTIVITY: It's Math Time

EQUIPMENT: A numbered grid on floor, canvas, oil cloth, etc. or numbers on non-slip squares arranged on floor.

EXPLANATION:

1. One child is IT and gives the class a problem to solve (Ex., 8 ÷ 2 = ?).

2. "Michael, you may be IT first. You may hop on one foot to get to any number or sign. For any number that is a part of the problem you should land on it with both feet for a few seconds."

3. After problem is hopped, "Class, what is the answer?"

HINTS:

1. Multiplication, addition, division and subtraction are possible.

2. The child acting as IT should be changed often.

3. Pupil response may be written or oral, individual or group.

Spelling

With the following spelling activities, children have the opportunity to translate a normally abstract experience into concrete terms. Within this activity section children learn to recognize words written on a board and with the help of classmates try to form the appropriate words with their bodies. Have them use their fingers to spell words in the sand, and play a relay race using letter cards. Other activities are directed toward the improvement of listening skills through games and spelling games in which children must physically move to and touch the letters of a word. All of these activities are intended to help children actually "experience" the spelling of words using as many of their senses as possible.

ACTIVITY: Listening Skills

SUGGESTED ACTIVITIES:

1. Children remain very quiet and try to identify all of the noises they hear both inside as well as outside the classroom.

2. Games designed to follow verbal directions: Simon Says, Follow the Leader, Listen and Do (stand up, hop on one foot, hop on both feet, sit down, etc.).

"Tell me what you hear."

3. Recitation of simple songs and nursery rhymes.

4. Identification of sounds using animal sounds, weather sounds, etc.

5. Following the instructions of a game on a musical record.

6. Children respond by imitating a series of hand claps, foot stomps, finger snaps or combination of each:
    2 claps 3 stomps 2 claps
    1 stomp 2 snaps 2 stomps, etc.

7.   Children close eyes and try to identify common sounds made by teacher: closing door, sliding chair, tapping pencil, etc.

8.   Children imitate human sounds: crying, laughing, singing, talking, etc.

9.   Children imitate weather sounds: wind, thunder, etc.

10.   Sounds are made on several rhythm instruments (drum, blocks, triangle, bell, etc.) as children watch. Children close eyes and try to identify the sounds as they are played one at a time. Next, two instruments can be played and identified as the first and last played.

ACTIVITY: Body Spelling

EQUIPMENT: Chalkboard and open floor space.

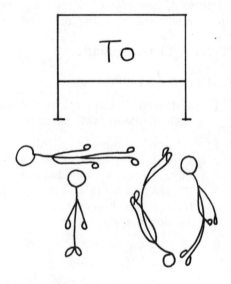

EXPLANATION:

1.   Divide your children into groups of three or more and arrange so they have open floor space.

2.   "I am going to write a word on the board. Using your bodies, I want you to form the letters on the floor."

HINTS:

1.   The size of the groups and the length of the words may be increased after the children have had sufficient practice.

2.   Teacher may call the word verbally rather than writing it.

ACTIVITY: Spell with a Bean Bag

EQUIPMENT: Letter grid, bean bag or similar object which can be pushed with the feet (the grid should contain all letters of the alphabet).

EXPLANATION:

1.   Each child may work alone at a grid or children may be divided into small groups.

2. "We are going to use your grid to let you spell. When I pronounce a word, push your bean bag to the first letter and touch the letter with your hand. Continue on to the second letter with your bean bag, touching it with your hand. Continue this until the word is spelled."

HINTS:

1. If more than one child is spelling, an observing child may be used to check the accuracy of the spelling.

2. Variation: A word may be written on the chalkboard by the teacher. A child then spells the word by moving to the appropriate letters on the grid. Care must be taken that there are sufficient letters on the grid to spell the word chosen.

3. Variation: Teacher calls letter sound and child runs to identify the letter which makes the sound. Some letters may be used more than once since they have different sounds.

4. Use different ways of moving on the grid.

Playground Activities

Balance

Balance is the ability to maintain your body in a stationary position either in a static or dynamic state. Standing on one leg is an example of static balance, and jumping on one foot across the room illustrates dynamic balance. Balance is one of the basic blocks upon which almost all physical education activities are built. Success in games, sport and dance depends, in part, on one's ability to maintain proper balance.

Developing good balance is very important for the child. It aids in acquiring smoothly coordinated and well controlled movements, which allows him to move with self-assurance—an important element in improving chances of success during playground and classroom activities.

ACTIVITY: Move and Freeze

EQUIPMENT: None.

EXPLANATION:

1. Children should be spread out over entire area.

2. "Can you walk very slowly all over the court without touching anyone? Remember to move to the open spaces and to freeze in a balanced position when the whistle blows."

HINTS:

1. Children may be asked to walk:
    —on tip toes
    —on heels
    —fast
    —lightly
    —heavy like an elephant
    —with long steps
    —backwards
    —sideways
    —forward
    —and freeze balanced on one body part when whistle blows
    —and freeze balanced on two body parts
    —and freeze balanced on three body parts
    —and freeze balanced on four body parts

EXPLANATION (cont.):

3. Same as #1, but ask children to run, skip, hop, slide, gallop, leap or jump using many of the variations listed in the HINTS above. Other variations are limitless but here are a few suggestions not listed above:
    When asked to run:
    —run like a deer
    —run in a straight line
    —run in a zig-zag line

    When asked to hop:
    —hop as high as they can
    —take short hops
    —take long hops
    —hop on one foot

When asked to skip:
—skip raising their knees very high
—skip around their partner
—skip as if they are jumping a rope

When asked to leap:
—leap from their right foot
—leap from their left foot
—run and leap
—leap over a line or small obstacle

When asked to jump:
—jump like a frog from one lily pad to another
—jump over a small box

ACTIVITY: Balance on Body Parts

EQUIPMENT: None.

EXPLANATION:

1. Can you balance on four parts of your body while we count to 10?" "Can you balance on four different parts?"

    HINTS:

    —knees and hands
    —knees and elbows
    —feet and hands

2. "Can you balance on three body parts while we count to 10?" "What other three parts can you balance on?"

    HINTS:

    —2 knees and 1 hand
    —2 hands and 1 knee
    —1 foot and 2 hands
    —head and knees
    —head and feet (only on mat)
    —1 elbow and 2 knees

3. "Can you balance on two body parts while we count to 10?" "Can you balance on 2 different parts?" "What other 2 parts can you balance on?"

HINTS:

—feet
—knees
—hands (on mat and with spotter)
—1 hand and 1 foot (same and opposite sides)
—1 knee and 1 hand (same and opposite sides)
—head and knee (on mat)

4. "Can you balance on one body part while we count to 5?" "What other part can you balance on?" "Can you think of another part?" Same but count to 10.

HINTS:

—right foot
—left foot
—right knee
—left knee
—seat

5. "Can you balance on four body parts while you move around the room?" "Change to 4 different body parts?"

6. Can you balance on three body parts while you move around the room?"

7. "Can you balance on two body parts while you move?"

8. "Can you balance on one body part and still move around the room?"

ACTIVITY: Walking a Tight-rope

EQUIPMENT: Line or tape on floor.

EXPLANATION:

1. "Let's pretend you are a tightrope walker in a circus. The tightrope is high in the air so you must be careful not to fall off. Put one foot right in front of the other one, use your arms to help you balance, and walk all the way to the end of the tightrope." "Now let's turn and walk back."

ACTIVITY: Balance Beam

EQUIPMENT: One balance beam (2" x 4" x 8') for 3 to 4 children

EXPLANATION:

1. "Have you ever seen a bird balancing and walking on a wire or a squirrel balancing and walking on a tree limb? Let's see if you can balance and walk like a bird or squirrel on this balance beam."

2. "Can you walk forward to the end of the balance beam without falling off? Remember to use your arms to help you balance and to look at the end of the beam as you walk."

   HINTS:

   —Teacher may want to have children walk a line on the floor first.
   —A long board lying flat on the floor may be another necessary progression.
   —The 4" side of the beam should be used first; as children progress, the 2" side may be used.

3. "Can you walk sideways to the end of the beam? Use your arms to help you balance."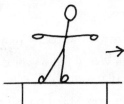

   HINTS:

   —The same progression as in #2 above.
   —Children should lead first with the right side and then with the left.

4. "Can you walk backwards to the end of the beam?"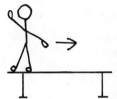

   HINTS:

   —Same progression as in #2 above.
   —Teacher may want to hold child's hand and walk beside him or let child put his hand on the teacher's arm as they walk.

5. "Can you walk to the end of the beam, turn around without falling off, and walk back?"

HINTS:

—Same progression as in #2 above.
—Encourage child to turn on the balls of his feet.

6.   ''Can you carry a ball in
      your right hand while you
      walk to the end of the beam?''

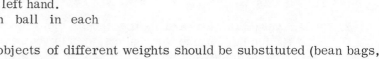

HINTS:

—Same progression as in
  #2 above.
—Same with left hand.
—Same with ball in each
  hand.
—Different objects of different weights should be substituted (bean bags,
  blocks, heavier balls, yarn balls, etc.)
—Put object on floor at mid-point of beam. Child walks to center, stoops,
  picks up the object and walks to end of beam.

ACTIVITY: Stork Stand

EQUIPMENT: None.

EXPLANATION:

1.   ''What is a stork?'' (explain if they do not know).

2.   ''Can you stand on your right
      foot like a stork?''

3.   ''Can you stand on your left
      foot?''

4.   ''Stand on your right foot
      and see if you can count to
      10 before you put your left foot down.''

5.   (Same with left foot.)

6.   ''Can you close your eyes and still stand very still on your right foot like
      a stork?''

7.   (Same on left foot.)

ACTIVITY: The Grasshopper

EQUIPMENT: Picture of a grasshopper or a live one in a jar.

EXPLANATION:

1.   ''Have you ever seen a
      grasshopper?''

2. "Show me how a grasshopper jumps up and down."

3. "Now let us pretend our grasshopper has only one leg. How would he jump then?"

4. "Can you move across the floor like a grasshopper?"

ACTIVITY: Jumping Boxes

EQUIPMENT: Jumping boxes made from wood or other sturdy material. They may also be made by taping the boxes, found in school cafeterias, containing six empty #10 size cans. The boxes are turned so that the opened ends are facing down; thus providing a firm support. The boxes should be painted in bright colors. One box may be used by itself or two boxes may be stacked and tied with heavy cord.

EXPLANATION:

1. Boxes should be scattered around floor.

2. "Stand behind a box. Can you step up on the box, jump into the air and land in a balanced position?" "Go on to the next box and do the same."

HINTS:

1. With younger children the boxes may be placed in front of the mats.

2. Children may be asked to move to the boxes using different locomotor movements: hop, slide, skip, run, walk, on all fours, crab walk, bear walk, elephant walk, etc.

3. "Jump in a different way from each box you come to." "Can you jump and turn in the air?" "Can you stretch your arms up high as you jump?" "Can you spread your feet apart and bring them together before you land?"

4. Boxes are placed in front of mats. "Can you jump from the box, land on your feet, roll on the mat and then stand up?: Remember, jump, land, roll, stand up."

ACTIVITY: High Kicking

EQUIPMENT: None.

EXPLANATION:

1. "Hold one arm out in front of you. Can you kick your foot up and touch your hand? Remember to keep your arm up when you try this. Now, try kicking with your other foot."

ACTIVITY: Donkey Kick

EQUIPMENT: Mat

EXPLANATION:

1. "Have you ever seen a donkey kick his back legs up in the air?"

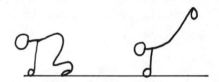

2. "Put your hands on the mat and see if you can kick your feet up like a donkey. Come down quickly after you kick your feet."

ACTIVITY: Spin the Top

EQUIPMENT: None.

EXPLANATION:

1. "Have you ever played with a top?" Explain how it works by showing a picture or bringing a top to class.

2. "See if you can jump straight up into the air and land in a balanced position."

3. "Hold up your right hand. Can you jump straight up and turn to the right while you are still in the air?" Same with left hand.

4. Teacher should stand facing children. "Can you jump and turn so that you land with your side to me? Freeze when you land. Can you jump and turn so that you land with your back to me? Freeze when you land. Jump and turn so that you land with your other side to me. Freeze. Can you jump and turn so that you land facing me?"

HINTS:

—Structures or environmental objects may be used, such as: land facing the school, land facing the field or the tree or the fence, etc.
—With older children fractions may be used: 1/4 turn, 1/2 turn, 3/4 turn.

5. "Can you jump and turn in a complete circle before you land? Remember, you should land facing in the same direction, as when you started the jump."

HINTS:

—Encourage children to use their arms to help them turn as well as for balance when landing, to bend the knees when they land, and to keep their feet spread slightly when they land.

ACTIVITY: "V" Seat

EQUIPMENT: None.

EXPLANATION:

1. "Sit down. Can you make a "V" with your hands? Can you raise your legs off the floor making a "V" with your body and your legs?"

   HINTS:

   —Child may place hands on floor for balance.
   —If a child can maintain this position, the next step is to ask him to grasp his knees

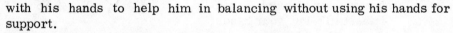

   with his hands to help him in balancing without using his hands for support.
   —Legs should be as nearly vertical as possible.

2. "Can you stretch your arms out straight over your legs? Can you hold your arms and legs very still while we count to ten?"

3. "Move your arms out to your side. Can you pretend you are a butterfly? Can you move your arms up and down?"

   HINTS:

   —Ask the child to lean to the right or left as he maintains his balance.
   —Some children will enjoy spreading arms and legs as they balance.

ACTIVITY: Shoulder Balance

EQUIPMENT: None.

EXPLANATION:

1.   Lie down on your backs, using your hands to support your hips.

2.   "Can you raise your legs up in the air?"

> HINTS:
>
> —Child should keep elbows and upper arms in contact with floor.

3.   "Can you hold your legs very still while we count to 10?"

4.   "Pretend you are riding a bicycle upside down. Can you pedal your bicycle first with one leg and then with the other. Can you make your bicycle go very slow, fast? How would you pedal your bicycle if you were going up a very high hill? Can you make your bicycle go backwards?"

ACTIVITY: Ball Balance

EQUIPMENT: Large rubber balls.

EXPLANATION:

1.   "Put your ball on the floor in front of you. Can you balance on your stomach on top of the ball? Put your hands on the floor to help you balance."

> HINTS:
>
> —The size of the balls used depend on the size of the children.

2.   "Can you balance on your stomach without using your hands?"

ACTIVITY: Balance Board

EQUIPMENT: Balance boards.

EXPLANATION:

1.   "Stand with your feet on either side of the balance board. Can you lean

so that the board tilts forward? Now regain your balance so you are standing
straight.''

HINTS:

—Use spotters for young
children.
—Start with large supports
under balance boards and
progress to smaller sup-
ports.

2. ''Can you lean so that the board tilts to the right? Now regain your balance so you are standing straight again.''

HINTS:

—Same but have child lean backward.
—Same but have child lean to the left.

3. ''Balance on your board so that it does not tilt. Once you are balanced,
stand very still. Can you touch your head with your hands while balancing?''

HINTS:

—Child could be asked to touch his:
nose, ears, eyes, mouth, chin, shoulders, elbows, hips, knees, toes,
neck, back, stomach.

4. ''Move your feet very carefully to the center of the board. Can you
balance on one foot without tilting the board? Try your other foot. Remember to move very slowly and very carefully.''

HINTS:

—Spotters should be used for this activity.

Coordination

Coordination is the harmonious functioning of the muscles into a skilled
movement pattern. This skilled movement may involve primarily eye-foot coordination (kicking a ball), eye-hand coordination (throwing a ball at a target),
symmetrical coordination (integration of both sides of the body—golf swing), or
overall coordination (swimming).

Good coordination is essential to successful performance in games, sport,
and dance. Of course, those movements which are more complex call for a
greater degree of coordination. Remember that in order to produce a well-coor-
dinated movement, the specific skills involved must be practiced many times.

Children can develop greater movement efficiency by practicing all types of coordination skills involving parts of, or the entire body.

The success of many classroom activities depend upon how well the child can make his eyes and hands work together. Examples are writing in a straight line, coloring within the lines, cutting with scissors, etc. Children need repeated opportunities to practice those skills developing proper eye-hand coordination, which is so important for learning success.

COORDINATION: EYE-HAND

ACTIVITY: Jump for the Wash

EQUIPMENT: Strips of cloth of different lengths attached to a strong cord. The cord may be strung between two standards or from one wall to another.

EXPLANATION:

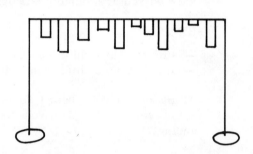

1.   "Stand under the clothes line. Now jump up and see how many pieces of the cloth you can touch. Can you touch the long pieces? Can you touch the short pieces too?"

HINTS:

1.   Cord should be strung at such a height that the long strips of cloth may be touched easily while the short ones present more of a challenge.

2.   Stress jumping straight up and not forward.

3.   For variety, old clothes may be used in place of the cloth strips. Old socks of different sizes, old shirts, old trousers, etc.

ACTIVITY: Wand Balance

EQUIPMENT: A wand for each child.

EXPLANATION:

1.   Children should be spread out around room with plenty of space between them.

2.   "Find the center or middle of your wand. Can you place the palm of your hand under the center of the wand and balance it? Try not to let it fall! Balance it the same way with your other hand."

3. "Stand the wand on end in the palm of one hand. Can you balance it so that it stays straight? Try not to let it fall! You will have to move your hand to keep it balanced and straight. Now try the same thing with your other hand."

4. "Can you drop the wand on one end and catch it after one bounce? Be sure to keep your eyes on it."

5. "Stand the wand on one end on the floor. Can you let go of it, turn yourself around one time, and catch it before it falls?"

6. "Can you walk around the room balancing the center of the wand in the palm of your hand? Can you walk around the room balancing the end of the wand in your palm?"

HINT:

1. Rubber grips may be placed on the ends of the wands for protection.

ACTIVITY: Hula Hoops

EQUIPMENT: One hula hoop for each child.

EXPLANATION:

1. Children should be spread out around room with plenty of space in between.

2. "Can you roll the hoop with your hand and keep it from falling over? Move all around the room with your hoop. Can you roll it with your right hand? Can you roll it with your left hand? Can you roll your hoop, run after it and catch it before it falls?"

3. "Get a partner. Put one of the hoops down. Can you roll the hoop back and forth to each other? Keep your eyes on it and try to catch it before it falls."

4. "Keep your partner. Each of you has a hula hoop. Can you roll the hoop back and forth to your partner while he rolls his hoop to you? Keep your eyes on both your partner's hoop and yours."

5. "Put your hula hoop on the floor. Can you walk around it? Can you walk in and out of your hula hoop? Can you walk with your right foot outside the hoop and your left foot inside the hoop? Can you jump into the hoop? Can you jump over the hoop?"

6. "Get a partner. Put one hoop down. One partner holds the hoop. Can you walk through the hoop? How many ways can you find to move through the hoop? Pick up the other hoop. What can you do with two hoops?"

7. "Can you roll your hoop away so it will come back to you?"

ACTIVITY: Balloon Volley

EQUIPMENT: Inflated balloons with a penny inside each balloon.

EXPLANATION:

1. Children should be spread out and each child should have a balloon.

2. "Can you throw your balloon into the air and catch it before it hits the ground?"

3. "Can you tap it lightly with both hands and keep it in the air. Keep tapping it to keep it up. Can you keep it up by tapping it with your right hand? Be sure to keep your eyes on the balloon. Can you keep it up by tapping it with your left hand? Alternate hands, tap it first with your right and then with your left. Keep your eyes on it."

4. "Get a partner and tap the balloons back and forth to each other."

5. "Can you tap your balloon lightly against the wall and keep it up?"

6. "Can you tap your balloon high into the air, turn around in a circle and catch it before it hits the floor?"

7. "Toss the balloon into the air and see how many times you can clap your hands before you catch it."

8. "Tap the balloon into the air. Can you touch your knees and catch the balloon before it hits the floor? Can you slap your thighs and then catch it? Can you touch your toes and then catch it? Can you clap your hands behind your back and then catch it?"

HINTS:

1. As skill improves, many of these activities may be done with bean bags or rubber playground balls.

2. The children should be encouraged to keep their eyes on the object being caught.

ACTIVITY: Suspendable Ball

EQUIPMENT: Wiffle balls, string, and paddles.

EXPLANATION:

1. Suspend a wiffle ball from the ceiling using a length of string. Ball should hang about shoulder high. There should be one ball for each child.

2. "Stand in front of your ball. Can you reach out and touch it with your fingers?"

3. "Can you hit it gently with your hand?"

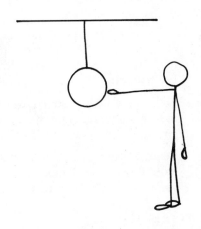

4. "Pick up a paddle. Can you hit the ball with the paddle? Remember to hit it gently and to keep your eyes on it."

5. "Start the ball moving gently. Reach out and poke it using your finger. Try to poke it each time it swings back to you."

6. "Push the ball to make it move. Can you stop it with your hand? Remember to keep your eyes on the ball."

7. "Start the ball moving. Can you hit it with your hand? Hit it each time it swings back to you. Count the number of times you hit the ball. Watch the ball."

8. "Start the ball moving. Pick up a paddle. Can you hit the ball with the paddle? Hit it each time it swings back to you. Count the number of hits you get. Remember to keep your eyes on the ball.

ACTIVITY: Bounce, Throw and Catch

EQUIPMENT: One playground ball for each child.

EXPLANATION:

1. Children should be spread out with plenty of space between them.

2. "Can you bounce the ball with one hand? Now try bouncing it with the other hand. Can you bounce it one time with your right hand and the next time with your left? Bounce the ball as low as you can. Bounce the ball as high as you can. Bounce the ball waist high."

3. "Can you throw the ball up and catch it before it bounces? Can you throw the ball up, let it bounce once and then catch it? Throw it up, let it bounce two times and catch it. Can you throw it up and catch it after the third bounce? Fourth bounce? Count how many times you can toss the ball up and catch it without letting it bounce."

4. "Put one of the balls down. Get a partner. Can you bounce the ball to each other? Can you roll the ball to each other? Toss the ball gently in the air to each other. Move a little farther away from each other and try bouncing the ball back and forth."

5. "Can you walk around while you bounce or dribble the ball? Dribble the ball with your right hand. Now try dribbling it with your left hand. Can you run slowly and still dribble the ball?"

6. "Get a partner. Each has a ball. Can you bounce your ball to your partner while he bounces his ball to you? You must keep your eyes on your partner's ball as well as yours."

ACTIVITY: Bowling

EQUIPMENT: Old bowling pins, plastic bowling pins, or plastic bottles, and balls.

EXPLANATION

1. Pins may be set up in a variety of patterns.

2. "Can you roll your ball and knock over the pins in front of you? Count the number of pins you knock over?"

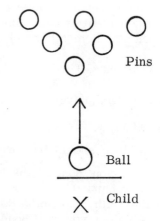

HINTS:

1. Start the children close to the pins so that every child is able to hit the pins successfully.

2. As skill improves increase the distance between the child and the pins.

3. Points may be scored for each pin knocked over.

ACTIVITY: Target Rotation

EQUIPMENT: Boxes of various sizes open at one end, #10 size cans empty and clean, and small necked plastic bottles for targets. Yarn balls, rubber jar rings, and bean bags for throwing. One or two commercial or homemade games such as indoor shuffleboard and horseshoes.

EXPLANATION:

1. Five or more target game stations set up around the play area. The children are divided into groups and each group is assigned a game. Groups rotate to different stations on signal.

2. Station set-up:

   Station #1: Three or four brightly painted boxes open at one end in a variety of sizes. Yarn balls for throwing. "Can you toss your yarn ball and make it land inside one of the boxes? Can you make it land inside the largest box? Can you make it land inside the smallest box?"

   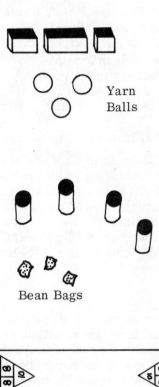

   Yarn Balls

   Bean Bags

   Station #2: Four or five empty #10 size cans painted in bright colors. Bean bags for throwing. "Can you throw your bean bag and make it land inside one of the cans? Can you make it land inside the closest can? Inside the can that is farthest away?"

   Station #3: Indoor shorty shuffleboard game.

   Station #4: Indoor horseshoe game (rubber horseshoes).

   Station #5: Four or five small necked platic bottles for targets. Rubber jar rings for throwing.

   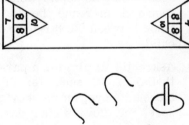

"Can you toss your rings and make them land over the neck of the bottles? Stand close to the bottles when you try this."

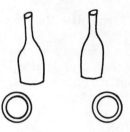

HINTS:

1. Target toss games either bought commercially or homemade are innumerable. The teacher should use available equipment and a lot of imagination.

2. Start with the children about five feet away from the targets. Increase the distance as skill improves.

ACTIVITY: Target Toss

EQUIPMENT: Large simple forms of animals, clowns, etc., cut from heavy cardboard or plywood. Holes of various sizes are cut out for the eyes, mouth, nose or in other places. The targets should be constructed with supports enabling them to stand alone, and can be painted in bright, attractive colors. Two to three bean bags for each child are needed.

EXPLANATION:

1. "Stand in front of one of the targets. Can you throw your bean bag and make it go through one of the holes in the target? Can you throw it through the big holes? Can you throw it through the little holes?"

HINTS:

1. Numbers may be painted by the large and small holes and scores may be kept. As skill improves increase the distance between the target and child.

2. Ask child to aim for a particular spot, such as: the elephant's eye, the monkey's nose, the clown's right ear, etc.

3. Targets may be hung from the ceiling at different heights.

4. Stress good basic throwing skills.

ACTIVITY: Variety Toss

EQUIPMENT: Heavy cord with a variety of objects spaced and tied on it. This cord may then be tied between two standards or from one wall to another.

EXPLANATION:

1. Children stand about 6 feet away from the objects on the cord and try to hit them with yarn balls, bean bags, or rubber playground balls.

Hoop   Wand   Bean Bag   Carpet Square

   HINTS:

   —Stress good throwing skills such as: use of opposite hand and foot, looking at the target, and follow through.
   —As skill improves have children back farther away before they throw at the targets.

2. "Count the number of objects you hit with your ball."

ACTIVITY: Games such as marbles, jacks, pick up sticks, checkers, Chinese checkers, sewing with a dull-pointed needle and yarn on burlap, or other games or activities stressing eye-hand coordination.

EQUIPMENT: Games or activities listed above which have been bought commercially or homemade.

EXPLANATION:

1. The games may be set up in stations around the room or outdoor area.

2. A system of rotation may be used to assure that every child has an opportunity to play each game.

HINT:

1. These activities may be set up indoors or outdoors.

COORDINATION: EYE–FOOT

ACTIVITY: Follow the Footprints

EQUIPMENT: Large paper footprints placed in a pattern on the floor.

EXPLANATION:

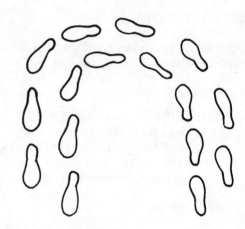

1. "These footprints belong to a big giant who came through here last night. Can you start here and walk in the giant's footprints?"

HINTS:

1. Different floor patterns may be used: geometric shapes, curved or straight paths, etc.

2. Footprints may be marked "right" and "left."

ACTIVITY: Walk and Jump the Rope

EQUIPMENT: Jump ropes scattered on floor around room. One rope for each child.

EXPLANATION:

1. "Let's pretend your rope is a very narrow bridge. Can you walk all the way to the end without falling off? Remember to use your arms to help you balance."

    HINTS:

    —Have children walk heel to toe.
    —Have children walk leading with right foot and sliding left up.
    —Same as above but lead with left and slide right.

2. "Now let us pretend that the rope is a tightrope in a circus. Can you walk the tightrope backwards?"

3. "The ropes are lying over an alligator pit now. See if you can walk sideways on the rope without falling in."

HINTS:

—Have children walk sideways leading with the right side.
—Same but lead with the left side.
—Same but cross one foot over the other.

4. "Let us use our ropes for jumping now. Pick them up and see if you can turn and jump them yourselves."

HINTS:

—One person at each end of a long rope. Swing the rope back and forth close to the ground. The child jumps it as it swings toward him.
—Have child stand in center with the rope on the outside. Swing it over child's head and have him jump it as it touches the ground.
—Teacher may have to give verbal commands telling child when to jump.

5. "Put your rope on the floor. Can you jump over it without touching it?"

HINTS:

—Have children jump back and forth over their own rope.
—Have children move around the room jumping over other ropes as they come to them.

ACTIVITY: Pathfinder

EQUIPMENT: Chalk or tape.

EXPLANATION:

1. Curved, zig-zag and straight paths are drawn or taped on the floor. Children are asked to move around the floor until they come to a path. The teacher gives verbal instructions as they move.

2. "Pretend you are an Indian walking through the woods. When you come to a path, see if you can walk forward on it without falling off. Walk forward on each path you find. Keep moving around the room looking for paths."

3. "Keep moving on the paths. Now see if you can walk backwards on the paths you find."

4. "Can you walk sideways without falling off?"

5. "Can you run on the paths?"

6. "See if you can skip on the paths."

7. "Show me if you can gallop on the paths."

8. "Can you slide on the paths?"

9. "See if you can move in a different way on each path. Can you change levels as you move?"

ACTIVITY: Walk the Challenge Course

EQUIPMENT: Hoops, tape, jump rope, balance beams, bean bags, wands or other available equipment.

EXPLANATION:

1. Children move through, around, over or on the objects.

HINTS:

1. Directions may be called out as children move through the course.

2. After skill improves, children may run through the course.

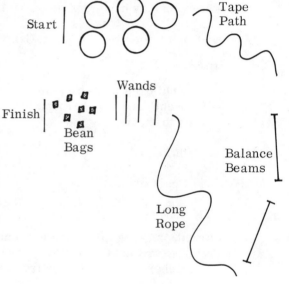

ACTIVITY: Hoop Walk

EQUIPMENT: Six to eight hoops.

EXPLANATION:

1. Hoops are placed in some pattern on the floor.

2. Children are in a line in front of the hoops. "Can you walk forward stepping into each hoop without touching it? Can you do the same thing walking backward? Can you walk sideways without touching them?"

3. "Can you walk on the right side of the hoops stepping with one foot inside the hoops and the other one outside?

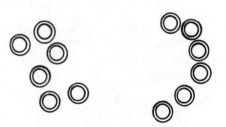

Walk back the same way on the other side of the hoops. Try not to touch them."

4. "Can you hop on one foot inside each hoop without touching it? Try the same thing on the other foot. Now try hopping on both feet."

HINT:

1. A variety of locomotor movements may be used in moving around or in-and-out of the hoops—skipping, running, sliding, galloping, leaping, jumping. Stress that the children move without touching the hoops.

ACTIVITY: Balloon Burst

EQUIPMENT: Two inflated balloons for each child and string.

EXPLANATION:

1. Two balloons are blown up and tied on the right and left ankles of each child. On a signal, the children try to burst each others balloons with their feet. The winner is the last child with an unbroken balloon.

2. Spread children out within the established boundaries. "When the whistle blows try to break everyone else's balloons by stepping on them, but try to keep yours from getting broken. Use only the feet and be very careful not to push anyone. The last one with an unbroken balloon is the winner."

ACTIVITY: Balloon Foot Volley

EQUIPMENT: A blown-up balloon with a penny inside for each child.

EXPLANATION:

1. "Lie down on your backs. Can you keep the balloon in the air using only your feet? How many times can you kick it before it touches the ground."

HINTS:

1. This activity should be done indoors as the slightest breeze makes it difficult to control the balloon.

2. Start out with giant balloons, as skill increases use smaller ones.

ACTIVITY: Hopscotch

EQUIPMENT: Hopscotch patterns painted or chalked on sidewalk or floor.

EXPLANATION:

1. Several different hopscotch patterns should be available to the children.

2. "Can you hop on one foot where there is one number or letter, and land on two feet where there are two numbers or letters side by side? Try not to touch the lines as you hop."

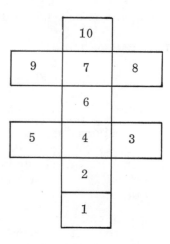

ACTIVITY: Toss the Bean Bag

EQUIPMENT: One bean bag for each child.

EXPLANATION:

1. " See if you can push the bean bag across the floor using first one foot and then the other. Keep the bean bag close to your feet as you move."

2. "Place the bean bag between your ankles or feet, can you jump it to your hands?"

3. "Place the bean bag on top of one foot, can you toss it into the air and catch it with your hands? Try tossing it with your other foot."

4. "Place the bean bag on the top of one foot, can you toss it into the air and make it land on top of your head?"

5. "Get with a partner. Put one of the bean bags down. Place the other one on top of your foot and toss it up so that your partner can catch it. Now let him toss it to you. Take turns tossing the bean bag back and forth. Be sure to try tossing it with your right and left foot."

ACTIVITY: Circle Kick

EQUIPMENT: One playground ball.

EXPLANATION:

1. Children stand in a circle and attempt to kick the ball between the other children and out of the circle.

2. "When the whistle blows try to kick the ball out of the circle. Keep the ball below shoulder height when you kick. Those in the circle should try to block the ball with their bodies to keep it from going out."

HINTS:

1. This game may be played with the children sitting in a circle and attempting to keep the ball inside by using only their feet.

2. Children may sit in two lines facing each other with legs outstretched. The ball is rolled between the two lines. The children from one line attempt to kick the ball over the heads of the children in the other line. Only feet may be used.

ACTIVITY: Getting a Kick out of Sports

EQUIPMENT: Soccer balls or rubber playground balls—one for each child. Cones or plastic bottles for obstacles.

EXPLANATION:

1. "Can you move the ball all around the floor using only your feet? Be sure to keep the ball close to your feet at all times. Tap the ball first with one foot and then with the other."

2. "Find a partner. Using only one ball, can you pass the ball back and forth to each other using only the feet. See if you can stop the ball using only one foot."

3. Scatter the cones all around the floor. "Can you dribble the ball with your feet between and around the cones without touching them? Try to keep your ball under control at all times."

4. Take children to playground. "Put the ball on the ground in front of you. Now kick it as hard as you can. Run after the ball and kick it again."

5. Spread children out on playground. "Hold the ball with both hands in front of you. Drop it and kick it before it hits the ground. This is called punting the ball. Can you punt the ball high into the air?"

6. "Drop the ball from both hands in front of you, let it bounce once and then kick it. Remember to keep your eyes on the ball."

ACTIVITY: Foot Bowling

EQUIPMENT: Old bowling pins or plastic bottles and playground balls.

EXPLANATION:

1. Pins are set up and children kick the ball in an attempt to knock them over.

2. "Can you knock the pins over by kicking the ball at them? Count how many pins you knock over. Try kicking the ball with your other foot."

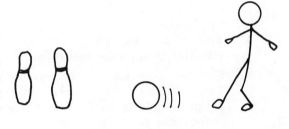

HINT:

1. Children should begin very close to the pins. As skill improves, increase the distance.

ACTIVITY: Soccer Croquet

EQUIPMENT: Objects set up around room through which or around which the ball may be kicked (open-ended boxes, hoops set on end, chairs, benches, cones, etc.)

EXPLANATION:

1. Children must move the ball using only the feet under, around, or through various obstacles.

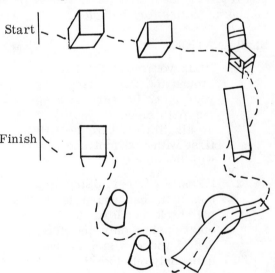

HINTS:

1. Encourage children to control the ball by kicking it gently through the course.

2. Encourage use of both right and left feet.

COORDINATION: SYMMETRICAL

ACTIVITY: Identification of Body Parts

EQUIPMENT: None

EXPLANATION:

1. The children touch various body parts in response to the teacher.
2. "Touch your ears with your hands."
3. "Point to your mouth."
4. "Put your hands over your eyes."
5. "Put your finger on your chin."
6. "Point to your nose."
7. "Touch your legs with your hands."
8. "Put your hands on your arms."
9. "Point to your elbow."
10. "Pat your stomach."
11. "Put your hands up in the air."
12. "Touch your knees with your hands."

HINT:

1. Repeat the above but ask children to respond with their eyes closed.

ACTIVITY: Movement of Body Parts

EQUIPMENT: None.

EXPLANATION:

1. The children move body parts in response to the teacher.
2. You may ask them to:
   —close their eyes   —wink their eyes
   —open their eyes   —squint their eyes

—close their right eye   —bend their necks
—close their left eye   —wiggle their toes
—clap their hands   —extend their arms
—wiggle their fingers   —extend their hands
—bend at the elbows   —open their hands
—bend at the knees   —wiggle their noses
—turn their heads   —shake their heads
—open their mouths   —nod their heads

ACTIVITY: Exploring Both Sides Through Movement

EQUIPMENT: None.

EXPLANATION:

1. The teacher presents a problem in the form of a question or statement and the children respond with appropriate movements.

2. "See if you can make small forward circles with your left arm. Now try the same thing with your right arm. Can you do the same thing going backward? Try both arms together."

3. "How high can you kick your right leg in front of you?" Left leg? Same to back.

4. "Can you move your right leg and right arm at the same time?" Left arm and leg. Right arm and left leg. Left arm and right leg.

5. "Can you hop forward on your right foot while you make circles with your right arm?" Same with left foot and arm. Right foot and left arm. Left foot and right arm.

6. "Lying on your back, can you move your right arm and leg at the same time?" Left arm and leg. Right arm and left leg. Left arm and right leg.

7. "Lying on your back, can you touch your right foot with your right hand?" Left foot with left hand. Right foot with left hand. Left foot with right hand.

HINT:

1. The variety of movements that may be presented to the children are almost limitless. With a little imagination and interest, the teacher can provide hours of creative and stimulating experiences for her children.

ACTIVITY: Exploring Both Sides with Balloons

EQUIPMENT: Two inflated balloons for each child. The balloons should be weighted with a penny or small pebble.

EXPLANATION:

1. The children should be spread out with one balloon for each child.

2. "Can you keep the balloon in the air using only your right hand?" Left hand.

3. "Will the balloon stay up if you tap it first with one hand and then with the other?"

4. "Can you keep two balloons in the air at the same time?"

5. "Lying on your back can you keep the balloon in the air using only your feet? Can you use your hands and feet together?"

6. "Kneel on both knees. Can you keep the balloon up using only your left hand?" Right hand.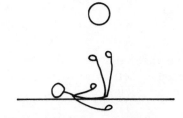

7. "Find a partner. Can you hit the balloon, back and forth using only the right hand?" Left hand. Right foot. Left foot.

8. "Can you hop on your right foot and at the same time keep the balloon up with your hands? Try the same thing hopping on your left foot."

HINT:

1. Many other movement combinations utilizing hands and feet may be used.

ACTIVITY: Exploring Both Sides With Balls

EQUIPMENT: One playground ball for each child.

EXPLANATION:

1. The children should spread out with plenty of room between them. Each child is given a ball.

2. "See how high you can throw the ball with your right hand." Left hand.

3. "Can you roll the ball to your partner using only the right hand?" Left hand?

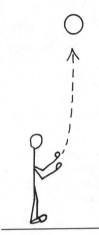

4. "See if you can keep your right hand on the ball and roll it all the way to the black line. Come back using your left hand."

5. "Toss the ball up with your right hand and catch it with your left hand." Change hands.

6. "Bounce the ball with your right hand." Left hand.

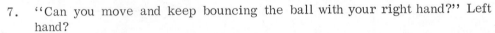

7. "Can you move and keep bouncing the ball with your right hand?" Left hand?

8. "See how many different ways you can throw the ball to your partner using your right hand." Left hand.

9. "Put the ball on the floor. Kick it softly to your partner with your right foot." Left foot.

10. "Can you walk and keep moving the ball with your right foot first and then your left foot?"

11. "Can you drop the ball from your waist and kick it with your right foot?" Left foot.

12. "Sit down facing your partner. See if you can roll the ball back and forth using only your right hand." Left hand.

13. Other combinations.

HINTS:

1. When working on symmetrical activities, always counter a movement or action using the right hand or foot with a movement or action using the left hand or foot.

2. Many of the above activities may be done with yarn balls or bean bags.

ACTIVITY: Tug of War

EQUIPMENT: Tug of war ropes—long and short.

EXPLANATION:

1. Children should be paired according to size. Each pair is given a tug-of-war rope.

2. "Take hold of the end of your rope. Keep the rope straight but do not begin to pull until the whistle blows. Bend your knees and use your whole body to help you pull."

   HINT:

   —The center of the rope should be marked with a piece of tape. This tape is then lined up over a line on the floor. The winner is the one pulling his opponent over the line.

3. Use a long rope tied together at the ends. Place the rope on the floor in the shape of a circle. The children spread themselves around the circle and behind the rope. The rope is picked up and held taut but no pulling begins until the signal is given.

4. Variations with a single tug-of-war rope with loops on the end:
   —"Can you pull your partner over the line using only your right hand? Now try using only your left hand."
   —"Can you pull better with both hands?"
   —"Sit down and hook the end of the rope over your right foot. On the signal, pull against your partner. Now try the same thing with your left foot."
   —"Grasp the rope with your right hand and with your body supported on three parts. Can you still pull against your partner? Try the same thing with your left hand."

   —"Stand back to back with your partner. Put the loop of the rope between your legs. Walk forward until the rope is taut. On the signal, pull against your partner."

ACTIVITY: Angels-in-the-Snow

EQUIPMENT: None.

EXPLANATION:

1. The children lie on their backs and move their arms and legs in response to the teacher. All movements should be done with the body parts in contact with the floor.

2. "Can you move your right arm up over your head? Bring it back to your side and try moving your left arm in the same way."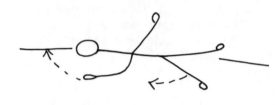

3. "How far can you move your right leg? Remember that your leg must touch the floor at all times. How far can you move your left leg?"

4. "Can you move your right arm and right leg together without raising them from the floor? Now try your left arm and leg."

5. "Can you move your right arm and left leg at the same time? How about your left arm and right leg?"

6. "Can you move both arms and legs at the same time? Remember to keep them in contact with the floor."

HINT:

1. With young children the teacher may have to point to the body part or parts to be moved.

ACTIVITY: Imitation of Postures

EQUIPMENT: None.

EXPLANATION:

1. The children stand in front of the teacher and attempt to imitate arm and leg movements.

2. "Can you move your arms and legs exactly like me? Be sure you look exactly as I do."

3. The possibilities are almost limitless but here are a few suggestions:

HINT:

1. After a little practice have the children get a partner with whom they will take turns imitating postures.

ACTIVITY: Magic Carpet Squares

EQUIPMENT: Carpet square on a smooth floor. One carpet square for each child.

EXPLANATION:

1. Spread carpet squares out around floor. The children go to a square and kneel on it.

2. "Can you slide yourself forward on your magic square using both hands together? Try the same thing going backward."

3. "Can you slide yourself forward using first one hand and then the other? Can you go backward the same way?"

4. "Lie on your stomach on your carpet square. Can you still slide yourself forward using both hands together? See if you can go backward the same way."

5. On stomach. "See how you would slide forward using first one hand and then the other. Now try it backward."

6. On stomach. "See how you would slide forward using both hands together, but pushing first with one foot and then with the other."

7. On stomach. "Can you slide forward using first your right hand and right foot together and then your left hand and foot?"

8. On stomach. "Can you move sideways on your magic square?"

9. "Sit on your square. Can you move now? In how many different directions can you move?"

HINT:

1. Scooter boards may be used in place of carpet squares.

Space and Direction

Once the child has developed an awareness of body image, he must be able to control his movements through space (surroundings), and to change the direction of his movements when necessary.

Through your guided learning experiences he should be given the opportunity to explore space through movement: backward, forward, sideways, right, left, etc. This exploration can also include different levels, speeds, and patterns of movement. Such teacher guiding statements as, "walk low to the ground, medium, high (levels in space); run quickly, slowly (speeds); skip a circle, square" (patterns) can be created to help a child explore space in meaningful ways.

Direction is another extremely important concept the child must master. This includes such direction as, "in front of, in back of, to the side, above, below, etc."

Through many movement experiences involving space and direction, the child will develop greater movement efficiency thus becoming more confident of his ability to manage his body in a variety of daily situations.

It is believed by many that an awareness of space and direction enables the child to read from left to right and to avoid letter reversals when writing (b for d, q for p, etc.).

ACTIVITY: Concepts

EQUIPMENT: 1 table, 2 chairs, 1 mat, 1 long rope, 1 short rope, 1 door, chalk circle on floor.

EXPLANATION:

1. Equipment should be scattered around area. The chairs should be placed so that the child can walk between them.

2. "Can you point up?"

3. "Can you point down?"

4. "Raise your right hand."

5. "Can you climb over the table?"

6. "Crawl under the table."

7. "Can you stand in front of a chair?"

8. "Stand behind a chair."

9. "Sit in a chair."

10. "Find a circle. Can you jump into the circle?"

11. "Can you jump out of the circle?"

12. "Lie down on the mat."

13. "Stand off the mat."

14. "Pick up the long rope."

15. "Find the short rope and pick it up."

16. "Can you place your feet above your head?"

17. "Place your hand below your knees."

18. "Find the circle. Can you walk around the circle?"

19. "Walk through the door."

20. "Can you walk between the chairs?"

ACTIVITY: Directional Course

EQUIPMENT: Chairs and wands

EXPLANATION:

1. Set up a directional course which will require the child to go over, under, between, and around certain obstacles.

2. "Can you step over the first wand? Can you go under the next wand? Can you walk between the chairs? Can you walk around the chair?"

HINT:

1. Other objects may be used for obstacles: tables, desks, cones and wands, etc.

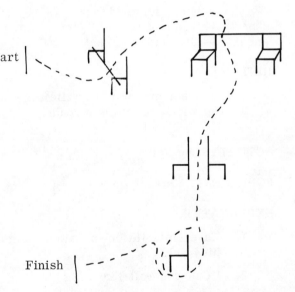

ACTIVITY: Listen and Do

EQUIPMENT: None.

EXPLANATION:

1. Children should be spread out around entire area. Give simple instructions for children to follow:
    —"Can you walk forward?"
    —"Can you walk backward?"
    —"Show me how you walk sideways."
    —"Can you skip forward?"
    —"Can you slide sideways?"
    —"Can you skip backward?"
    —"Gallop forward."
    —"Hop forward."
    —"Can you hop backward?"
    —"Hop sideways to the right."
    —"Hop sideways to the left."
    —"Can you leap forward?"
    —"Jump forward."
    —"Jump backward."
    —"Jump to the side."

HINT:

1. Teacher may want to write some directions on flash cards and hold them up for the children to read:

ACTIVITY: Log Roll

EQUIPMENT: Mats.

EXPLANATION:

1. Have child lie on his stomach at one end of the mat with his hands over his head.

2. "Can you roll like a log all the way to the end of the mat? Try to roll straight down the mat. Be sure to keep your eyes open."

HINT:

1. Spotter should be at child's head to prevent him from rolling onto the floor and hitting his head.

ACTIVITY: Space Walk

EQUIPMENT: Sidewalk or other open area on which patterns may be painted.

EXPLANATION:

1. Directions may be painted beside each floor pattern, such as: hop right, hop left, etc. Children start at the beginning and follow the painted space walk.

HINTS:

1. The space walk may include anything the teacher deems necessary.

2. If directions are placed on movable cones instead of being painted on the sidewalk, the space walk may be changed periodically.

3. Children unable to read may be talked through the space walk by the teacher.

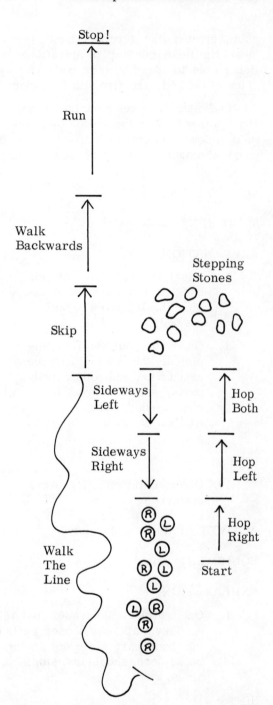

Body Image

It is believed that a good body image is basic to the development of perceptual-motor skills. Through guided participation in physical activities, children can explore and discover how their bodies are capable of moving. "How high can you jump, stretch like a rubber band, how big can you be," are only three of the almost limitless number of questions you can ask your children to respond to. Being able to identify their body parts and distinguish between the right and left sides of the body are also vitally important.

Individual achievement levels are inseparable from how each person feels about himself. For the child, then, this becomes crucial. As the teacher you are in a unique position to help each one of your children discover their individual physical uniqueness in a positive and encouraging way.

ACTIVITY: Body Outline

EQUIPMENT: None.

EXPLANATION:

1. Have the child lie on his back on a large sheet of paper. Use a crayon to outline his body.

2. Once the outline is completed, the child may be asked to add other body parts, such as eyes, ears, nose, mouth, fingers, etc. Clothes may be colored in also.

HINT:

1. Older children may draw around each other.

ACTIVITY: Follow the Leader

EQUIPMENT: None.

EXPLANATION:

1. One child is the leader and is followed in a line by the other children. As they walk, the leader calls out a body part. The children must touch the body part while continuing to walk. The leader may call out: ears, neck, nose, shoulders, stomach, knees, ankles, elbows, head, back, legs, arms.

HINTS:

1. The leader should be changed frequently.

2. Arm positions and movements may be practiced in the same way: right arm up, left arm up, both arms up, both arms extended, both arms swinging, etc.

ACTIVITY: Contacting Body Parts with Available Objects or Other Body Parts

EQUIPMENT: None.

EXPLANATION:

1. "Touch your knees to the floor."
2. "Touch your hands to the floor."
3. "Can you make your elbows touch your knees?"
4. "Can you touch your hand to your wrist?"
5. "Stand so that your arms are touching your sides."
6. "Can you make your nose touch the floor?"
7. "Touch your foot to your head."
8. "Stand so that your heels are touching the wall."
9. "Make your knee touch your chin."
10. "Hold your ankles with your hands."
11. "Can you kneel and put your ear on the seat of the chair?"

HINTS:

1. Use objects that are easily available.
2. Many other variations are possible.

ACTIVITY: Simon Says

EQUIPMENT: None.

EXPLANATION:

1. Play "Simon Says," but use the movements of specific body parts as commands. Simon says:
   —"bend your elbows
   —snap your fingers
   —close your eyes
   —open your mouth
   —shrug your shoulders
   —put your hands on your knees
   —stamp your feet
   —stand on tip-toes
   —clap your hands
   —point to your nose, etc."

HINT:

1. Use a child to play the part of "Simon Says." Change the leader frequently.

ACTIVITY: Shadow Designs

EQUIPMENT: Opaque projector, movie projector, or other light source.

EXPLANATION:

1. Aiming the light from the projector against a wall, have the child step in front of the light creating shadows.

2. "Make your shadow as big as you can."

3. "Make it as small as you can."

4. "How tall can you make your shadow?"

5. "How short can you make it?"

6. "Can you make your shadow very wide?"

7. "Can you make it very narrow?"

8. "Pretend you are a bird. Can you make your shadow look like a bird?" Same but use other animals: elephant, monkey, dog, etc.

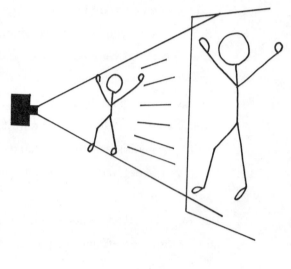

9. "How can you make your shadow move?"

10. "Move only your fingers. How many different ways can you move them. Keep watching your shadow as you move them in many ways." Same, but move only: arms, head, legs, and feet.

11. "How many different ways can you make your arms bend? What part of your arm bends? (elbow) Can you make your arms bend at the elbow and then stretch them out again? Watch your shadow as you move. "Same, but with legs (bend at the knee), head (bend at the neck), feet (bend at the ankle), hands (bend at the wrist), body (bends at the hips).

12. "Can you make a design with your shadow? What else can you make your shadow do? Can it jump up? Can it hop? Can it walk? Can it run in place? Can it leap? Can it skip?"

13. "See what else your shadow can do."

ACTIVITY: Human Stick Figures

EQUIPMENT: None

EXPLANATION:

1. Six children work together to make the shape (with their bodies) of a human stick figure lying on the floor.

2. At first, parts may be assigned: "Paul, you be the head."; "Mary, you be the right arm." etc.

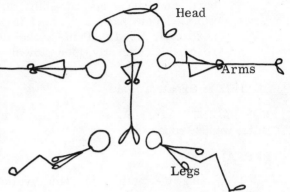

3. Once the body is made, the parts may move. "Mary, you are the right arm. Can you make it stretch? How else can you make the arm move?" Same with other children.

4. You may ask the children to respond to commands such as: "Bend the right leg. Raise the right arm. Bend the left arm."

ACTIVITY: Body Jump

EQUIPMENT: Chalk or tape.

EXPLANATION:

1. A large stick figure of a man is drawn or taped on the floor for each child. The children are asked to hop or jump from one body part to another.

2. "Can you stand on the head and jump to the neck?"

3. "Can you jump from the neck to the right hand?"

4. "Jump from the right hand and see if you can land on the waist."

5. "Can you jump from the waist to the left hand?"

6. "Now try jumping from the left hand to the left foot."

7. "See if you can jump from the left foot to the right foot."

8. "Stand on the right foot. Can you walk up the right leg, jump to the head, and then walk backwards to the left foot?"

9. "Stand on the right hand. Can you hop on one foot to the left hand?" Many other variations are possible and should be used.

10. "Stand in front of your stick figure. I will call out the name of a body part, and you run and stand on it as fast as you can. When I blow the whistle come back and stand in front of your stick figure ready for the next call. Head." Pause long enough to be sure that every child has responded correctly, then blow the whistle. "Leg," etc.

ACTIVITY: Create a Body

EQUIPMENT: A variety of available materials: bean bags, boxes, cans, hoops, balls, wands, ropes, etc.

EXPLANATION:

1. Using the materials made available by the teacher, the children build a body on the floor.

2. "Can you build a human body using the boxes, hoops, cans, bean bags, and other materials you see here?"

    HINT:

    —The older children may be given time to experiment on their own, but it may be necessary to guide the younger children by saying: "Look at all of this equipment. Can you see something that would make a good head? What comes after the head? Can you see something we could use for the neck?" Same for other body parts.

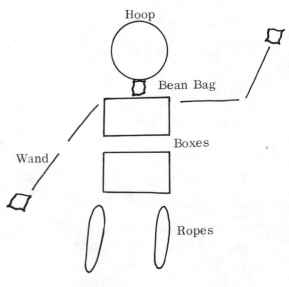

3. When the children have finished, ask them to study the body they created for several minutes. Afterward, take the different parts, stack them in a pile and see how quickly they can put the body back together again. For added interest let the children give their body a name (Fred, Sam, Hazel, etc.). "Let us take 'Sam' apart and stack him in a pile. When the whistle blows, see how fast you can put 'Sam' back together again."

4. Using old clothes and other available materials, help your children make a three dimensional straw man to keep in the classroom.

Rhythm

Rhythm fulfills an inherent need in children of all ages. It serves as an exciting opportunity for creative self-expression through freedom of movement. Through rhythm, a child can experience the joy and exhilaration of moving in time to the beat of a drum, the ring of a tambourine, or the tempo of a record.

Through fundamental rhythms each child learns to move effectively and efficiently by integrating different body parts into a smooth functioning whole. He develops a feeling of grace and poise which serve to enhance feelings of self in relation to his capabilities.

Rhythm is an area of the curriculum in which all children can meet with success. It provides another opportunity for positive self-expression and growth in a most desirable manner.

ACTIVITY: Make Believe World

EQUIPMENT: Suitable accompaniment depending on the individual situation.

EXPLANATION:

1. Individually or in small groups, children make believe that they are other people, animals, plants, machines, weather conditions, etc.

2. "Pretend you are soldiers. How do soldiers march?"

3. "You are the pilot of a big jet airplane. Can you show me some of the things you would do? Can you take off in your plane? Can you land it?"

4. "Let's pretend you are monkeys in the jungle. Show me how monkeys move." Same with other animals like elephants, tigers, dogs, snakes, ducks, etc.

5. "A spell has been cast and you have all been changed into witches! Show me how you would act. How do witches fly?"

6. "Now you are monsters from another world. How would you move?"

7. "Pretend you are a train. Can you go forward? Can you go backward? How does a train move going up a big, steep mountain? How does it move coming down the mountain?"

8. "Have you ever ridden in a big truck? Pretend you are driving the truck. How would you move? Can you drive the truck on a winding mountain road? How does a truck sound?"

9. "Let's make believe that you are the leaves on a big tree. How do the leaves move when the wind blows? What happens to leaves that have been blown down? Do they move when the wind blows? How do they move?"

10. "There is a terrible storm coming our way. First comes the wind. Can you move like the wind in a storm? Next comes the rain. What does rain look like? Then the lightning flashes in the sky. Now you are the lightning." Children may be divided into three groups and act out the storm together. One group acts out the wind, one the rain, and one the lightning.

ACTIVITY: The Orchestra

EQUIPMENT: None.

EXPLANATION:

1. Small groups of children (4-5) choose an instrument to imitate. They may imitate it in terms of its shape, sound, and movement. (Example: one group may choose a drum, another a violin, another a guitar.) Each group practices and then performs for the rest of the children who try to guess what instrument they were imitating.

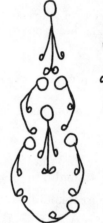

Bow-
Child moves over other children and makes sound of violin.

HINTS:

1. You may want to provide each group with a picture of the instrument they chose and discuss some of its qualities—how it moves, what sound it makes, etc.

2. Use a simple tune or song for all groups, such as Twinkle, Twinkle Little Star. Each instrument would then play the same tune.

3. After the instruments have been presented to the group and identified, the entire class may perform the tune together making a symphony orchestra.

ACTIVITY: Dramatization of Creative Rhythms

EQUIPMENT: None.

EXPLANATION:

1. Individually or in small groups children dramatize:
    —The interpretations of familiar stories or nursery rhymes such as The Three Bears, Little Red Riding Hood, The Three Little Pigs, Mary Had A Little Lamb.
    —Playing sports activities such as basketball, boating, tennis, golf, archery, football, swimming, track and field, hockey, etc.
    —Making a snowman. "Pretend it is snowing; can you gather some snow and make a big snowman? What parts does a snowman have? Can you make those parts out of snow?"

—Flying a kite. "It is a very windy day and you are flying a kite. How strong is the wind today? Show me. Hang on to your kite string; can you feel the kite pulling you?"

—Climbing a mountain. "The mountain is steep and you have to crawl up it very slowly. Can you make it to the top?"

—In the woods. "Let us skip down this trail in the woods—can you climb up on this tree branch and jump down—here comes a big bear. Let us run!"

—Building a house. "We need some big boards for our house. Can you pick up the boards and make the walls? Hammer the nails into the wood so the walls stay up. Let us all help put on the roof and nail it down. Can you paint the house?"

—Shopping in a grocery store. "You are going shopping in a grocery store with your mother. Can you show me how you shop?"

HINTS:

1. Records may be used for accompaniment, or a tape may be recorded to fit the music to the dramatization.

2. The class may be divided into groups with each group practicing on its own and then presenting their dramatization to the rest of the class.

3. The children may want to construct simple props to aid in the presentation of the dramatization.

ACTIVITY: Move to the Drum (this activity should be used when presenting a particular beat [4/4, 6/8, etc.] to the children for the first time).

EQUIPMENT: Drum.

EXPLANATION:

1. The teacher uses a basic beat on the drum and helps them to understand it and feel it.

2. "Sit down and listen to the beat. Can you count the beat with me?"

3. "Let us clap hands to the beat of the drum."

4. "Clap your hands loudly on the accented beat and softly on the unaccented beats."

5. "Can you change the position of your arms on the accented beat and hold that same position on the unaccented beats?" Same with one arm, one foot, two feet, etc.

6. "Can you change the position of your arms on every beat?" Same with feet.

Standing

7. "Can you stamp your foot to the beat of the drum? Stamp it loudly on the accented beat and softly on the unaccented beat."

8.   "Move your arms in a different position on each beat." Same with legs.

9.   "Can you move your body parts in unison (together) to the beat? Can you move first one body part and then another to the beat of the drum?"

10. "Make a body shape on the accented beat and hold it on the unaccented beats."

Moving

11. "Can you walk to the beat of the drum?"

12. "Walk to the beat of the drum but bend your knees on every accented beat." Same but touch floor on accented beat.

13. "Can you walk and clap your hands to the beat?"

14. "Move to the beat. As you move change the position of your arms on every accented beat."

15. "The tempo is going to get faster so now you must move faster. Listen to the beat as you move." Same but slow down the tempo.

ACTIVITY: Band Member

EQUIPMENT: A variety of percussion instruments: drums, sticks, tambourines, cymbols.

EXPLANATION:

1.   Divide the children into groups with four to five children in each group.

2.   "Each person in each group choose an instrument you would like to play as you march with your group around the room."

HINTS:

1.   At first, let the children beat out any rhythm they wish as they move around the room.

2.   Assign a beat to each group, 2/4, 3/4, 4/4.

3.   Assign a band leader and line the children up behind him as they march.

ACTIVITY: The Body with a Beat

EQUIPMENT: Drum or other percussion instrument.

EXPLANATION:

1.   Select a beat, demonstrate and explain it to the children.

2.   In response to the beat ask the children to:
     —"Put both hands on your: head head head head/ ears ears ears ears/

nose nose nose nose/ toes toes toes toes (same with other combinations of body parts)

—Put both hands on your: head/ears/nose/toes

—Sit and put your head on your; arm arm arm arm/ leg leg leg leg/
knee knee knee knee/ foot foot foot foot.'' (Same with other body parts
in different combinations.)

—''I will now ask you questions about what your body parts do and you
can tell me.'' (Teacher asks: eyes–eyes–eyes–eyes/ children answer:
see–see–see–see). Same using: ears–hear, nose–smells, mouth–talks,
feet–walk, hands–touch.

HINT:

1.   Use other beats or rhythms.

ACTIVITY: Concepts with a Beat

EQUIPMENT: Drum or other percussion instrument.

EXPLANATION:

1.   The teacher selects the beat to be used, in this case 4/4, explains it,
     and asks the children to respond by moving a part or parts of their
     bodies.

2.   ''Move your right arm: up up up up/down down down down.'' Same with
     left arm, both arms, right and left legs, and combinations of arms and
     legs.''

3.   ''Make your body: big big big big/small small small small.''

4.   ''Stand so that you are: wide wide wide wide/narrow narrow narrow
     narrow.''

5.   ''Reach with your arms: high high high high/low low low low.''

6.   ''Move your arms: open open open open/closed closed closed closed.''
     Same with legs.

7.   ''Walk: forward forward forward forward/backward backward backward
     backward.''

8.   ''Make yourself: tall tall tall tall/short short short short.''

HINTS:

1.   For variety use another rhythm:
     tall tall/short short
     up up/down down
     high high/low low

2.   For more rapid movement try combining concepts:
     tall short/tall short
     up down/up down
     wide narrow/wide narrow

ACTIVITY: Move to the Beats

EQUIPMENT: Various types of percussion instruments: drums, sticks, tambourines, others.

EXPLANATION:

1. Divide the children into groups with four to six children in each group.

2. Designate a leader who selects one of the instruments. He then beats out a rhythm and the other children in the group respond by moving to the beat.

3. The following ideas may be stressed:
   —Use locomotor movements of his own choice
   —Use non-locomotor movements of own choice
   —Entire group moves in unison
   —Move with a partner
   —Group plays follow-the-leader
   —Designate locomotor movements: walk, run, skip, etc.
   —Designate non-locomotor movements: swinging, turning, swaying, bending, etc.

HINT:

1. This activity should be used only after the children have gained some confidence in moving to basic beats or rhythms such as 2/4, 3/4, 4/4.

ACTIVITY: Moving to Music

EQUIPMENT: Record player and various records. Any music may be used, but it should have an easily defined, definite beat. Children enjoy moving to modern music.

EXPLANATION:

1. In response to the rhythm of the music, have your children perform the following movements:
   —"Can you walk, run, skip, gallop, slide, hop, jump.
   —Move with your body in a high position while going left, right. (Can use medium and low body positions and various directions while walking, hopping, running, etc.)
   —Clap your hands to the beat of the music.
   —Using your feet, stamp to the beat.
   —Swing your arms to the music (big and small movements).
   —Bend and stretch in time with the music."

HINT:

1. At first, children should be seated and listening while the teacher explains the rhythm or beat. Next, by clapping or moving an isolated body part children should demonstrate that they hear and understand the beat or rhythm.

Appendix

The field of perceptual-motor learning offers a wide selection of teaching aids, films, filmstrips, records and books. Several publishers and educational organizations were contacted to determine what materials were available for the teacher who was interested in perceptual-motor learning. The selected sampling is far from exhaustive and at best is representative. Descriptive comments of materials were taken from publishers explanatory comments and from a personal review of materials. A brief descriptive comment and where to order each item it included.

Books

Audio-Visuo Motor Training with Pattern Cards by Edith Klasen aids in the remediation process for children whose learning was impaired because of neurosensory disorders in such areas as visual perception, motor control, auditory functions and lateral dominance. Problem learners in the classroom often have mixed dominance; difficulties in right-left orientation; spatial relationships and balance; deficient motor functions or poor eye-motor coordination; reversal tendencies; or poor auditory memory or lack of auditory discrimination. Peek Publications, P. O. Box 11065, Palo Alto, Ca. 94306.

Daily Sensorimotor Training Activities by William J. Braley, Geraldine Konichi and Catherine Leedy. This is a handbook for teachers and parents to increase perceptual awareness and motor ability of preschool and primary children. Activities are divided into the areas of body images, space and direction, balance, basic body movement, hearing discrimination, symetrical activities, eye-hand coordination, eye-foot coordination, form perception, rhythm, large muscle, fine muscle and games. Educational Activities, Inc., Freeport, L.I., N.Y. 11520.

Integrated Development: Motor Aptitude and Intellectual Performance by A.H. Ismail and Joseph J. Gruber offers evidence to demonstrate the relationship between perceptual-motor and intellectual development. The motor variables, coordination, balance and kinesthetics are indicators of intellectual proficiency. Controlled experiments attempt to define the relationships between motor and

147

mental abilities. Charles E. Merrill Pub. Co., 1300 Alum Creek Drive, Columbus, Ohio 43216.

Junior Listen-Hear Books by Jan Slepian and Ann Seidler is a developmental program of five books written to develop auditory discrimination in younger children. The set of five books, teacher's source book, recording and set of 3 posters (PS-2) are available from: Follett Publishing Co., P.O. Box 5705, Chicago, Ill. 60680.

A Guide to Movement Exploration by Layne C. Hackett and Robert C. Jensen is a practical teaching guide which explores the creative approach to teaching physical education, reading readiness and the educationally handicapped. Peek Publications, P.O. Box 11065, Palo Alto, Ca. 93406.

Listen-Hear Books by Jan Slepian and Ann Seidler is a new approach to speech understanding. This series includes six books written by speech therapists to help develop auditory discrimination of troublesome letter sounds . . . L, F, K, R, S, and TH. The six books and teacher's source book (K-3) are available from: Follett Publishing Co., P.O. Box 5705, Chicago, Ill. 60680.

Movement Exploration and Games for the Mentally Retarded by Layne C. Hackett emphasizes the problem solving approach in physical education activities. The attention focuses on the development of a positive attitude toward movement which should encourage the child to seek physical activity and dynamic living. Peek Publications, P.O. Box 11065, Palo Alto, Ca. 93406.

Movement, Perception and Thought by Bryant J. Cratty offers planned movement experiences as a learning channel. Very often, the desire of a child to move interferes with academic achievement in the classroom. Many of the suggested activities in this book should help the child to control his movements, reducing hyperactivity and increasing attention span. Peek Publications, P.O. Box 11065, Palo Alto, Ca. 93406.

Teaching One Child by Ernest Seigel is a theoretical and practical book on how to sequentialize instructional tasks and take advantage of feedback, how to understand wrongness and employ it for rightness, how to individualize instruction and the role of the parent. Educational Activities, Inc., Freeport, L.I., N.Y. 11520.

The Purdue Peceptual-Motor Survey by Eugene G. Roach and Newell C. Kephart provides the teacher with a tool which can be used to identify those children who do not possess the perceptual-motor abilities necessary for acquiring academic skills by the usual instructional methods. Charles E. Merrill Pub. Co., 1300 Alum Creek Drive, Columbus, Ohio 43216.

Teach and Reach That Child by Eleanor Cochran to help the teacher in the early identification of learning problems. Curriculum is organized into broad areas of sensory and perceptual development. Suggestions for curriculum adoption and materials utilization and teaching procedure are defined. Peek Publications, P.O. Box 11065, Palo Alto, Ca. 93406.

Films

Blocks . . . A Medium for Perceptual Learnings is a 16mm film with sound and color. This 17-minute film focuses on the perceptual learnings that are inherent in block building, derived from how a child perceives the blocks with which he works and the space in which he builds. The perceptual learnings are further detailed in relation to academic learnings. Campus Film Distributors Corporation, 20 E. 46th Street, New York, N.Y. 10017.

Bridges to Learning is a 16 mm, 30 minute sound and color film which depicts a kindergarten through sixth grade physical education program. Perceptual-motor activities are emphasized. Palmer Films, Inc., 611 Howard Street, San Francisco.

Creative Body Movements is a 16mm 11 minute color and sound film which shows primary children involved in perceptual-motor activities. Martin Moyer Productions, 900 Federal Ave. East, Seattle, Wn. 98102.

Discovering Rhythm is a 16mm 11 minute, sound and color film which depicts rhythm as an outgrowth of activities such as walking and running. Basic concepts related to rhythm are discussed. Universal Education and Visual Arts, 221 Park Avenue South, New York, N.Y. 10003.

Movement Exploration is 16mm 20 minute sound and color film which shows activities for Kindergarten through sixth grade children. The wide range of movement activities involves the child in the problem solving approach. Documentary Films, 3217 Trout Gulch Rd., Aptos, Ca. 95003.

Movement Education: What Am I? is a 16mm, 11 minute, color and sound film which shows children how to use their bodies to move in various ways. Film Associations, 11559 Santa Monica Blvd., Los Angeles, Ca. 90025.

Moveginic Curriculum is a 16mm 30 minute, black and white film which depicts a perceptual-motor activity curriculum for the educationally disadvantaged child. University of Wisconsin Bureau of Audio-Visual Instruction, University Extension, 1312 West Johnson, Madison, Wisc. 53701.

Moving is Learning is a 16mm color and sound 18 minute film which shows perceptual-motor retraining techniques used by a visual learning center to assist perceptually handicapped children. Canadian Association for Children with Learning Disabilities, Suite 322, 88 Eglinton Ave., East Toronto 315, Ontario, Can.

Outdoor Play . . . A Motivating Force for Learning is a 16mm film with sound and color. This 17-minute film presents the unique physical and intellectual development provided by outdoor play activities and the extensive use of improvised materials. The child interacts with various materials and with each other in exploration of space, experimentation with balance, development of muscular coordination and body awareness. Developmental differences are related and self-determined activities and goals are shown. Campus Film Distributors Corp., 20 E. 46th St., New York, N.Y. 10017.

Perc! Pop! Sprinkle! is a 16mm color and sound 11 minute film which gives visual experiences for children to observe and then to express through movement. Martin Moyer Productions, 900 Federal Ave. East, Seattle, Wn. 98102.

Piaget's Developmental Theory I—Conservation #7121 is a 28-minute color film which demonstrates the stages of the development of thinking in children and how to assess these with Piaget's theories. Children, ages 5-12, are presented tasks involving conservation of quantity, length, area and volume. The characteristics of thought from pre-operational to form are identified. University of California Extension Media Center, Berkeley, Ca. 94720.

Piaget's Developmental Theory II—Classification #7120 is a 17-minute color film which shows children at several developmental stages responding to tasks of differing mental operations essential to classification. University of California Extension Media Center, Berkeley, Ca. 94720.

Piaget's Developmental Theory: IV Growth of Intelligence in the Preschool Years #8327 is a 30-minute color film which examines growth of thinking processes in the preschool years. Children ages 3-6, are presented with tasks that reveal how they think as they sort objects, place them in one to one correspondence or arrange them according to size. University of California Extension Media Center, Berkeley, Ca. 94720.

Readiness for Reading is a 16mm sound film in color which explains the desirability and necessity for five areas of reading readiness: perceptual, experiential, language, interest, and social-emotional. The teacher is shown ways to develop each area. Educational Motion Pictures, Indiana University, Audio-Visual Center, Bloomington, Ind. 47401.

Thinking, Moving, Learning is a 16mm 20-minute color and sound film which depicts perceptual—motor activities for Kindergarten and Primary grade children. Bradley Wright Films, 390 N. Duane, San Gabriel, Ca. 91775.

Why Physical Education is a 16mm 14-minute sound and color film which depicts the importance of physical education in developing hand, foot and eye coordination which helps the mind and body to work together more effectively. The value of physical education in developing strength, flexibility, and endurance is identified. Audio-Visual Center, Indiana University, Bloomington, Ind. 47401.

Filmstrips

Approaches to Learning suggests practical classroom techniques for developing in young children the basic perceptual—motor, and cognitive skills which are prerequisite to academic success. This series provides a general background and understanding of the basic skills areas and their relationship to academic learning. Three filmstrips with records or cassettes are available from Teaching Resources, 100 Boylston Street, Boston, Mass. 02116.

Developing Cognitive Skills in Young Learners in a series of filmstrips designed to help the child in the development of fundamental intellectual concepts such as ordering, grouping and inferring. The child is helped in acquiring many of the perceptual and cognitive skills necessary for intellectual growth. Seven color filmstrips and guide from Educational Activities, Inc., Freeport, L. I., N. Y. 11520.

54 Functional Words uses a multisensory approach—visual, kinesthetic and tactile—in teaching the functional words and signs of everyday life to primary classes. This series includes 9 color filmstrips, 54 flashcards, 64 page workbook and teacher guide from Warren Schloat Productions, Pleasantville, N. Y. 10570.

Making Logical Judgements is a series of filmstrips designed to help the child develop fundamental intellectual concepts which are crucial to school learning. Experiences are offered to train the child in multiple categorization, relational concepts, visual comprehension, ability to recognize logical inconsistencies, and logical analysis. Seven color filmstrips and guide from Educational Activities, Inc., Freeport, L. I., N. Y. 11520.

Perceptual Skills is a series of six filmstrips: Basic visual perceptions: color, form, size; perception of sound; perception of spatial relationships; figure ground discrimination; perception of parts to whole relationships; and perception of sequence. Activities of matching, recognizing, sorting and relative size, as well as activities to develop the concept of constancy are presented. Six filmstrips with records or cassettes from Teaching Resources, 100 Boylston Street, Boston, Mass. 02116.

Phrase Training Filmstrips Grade K-6 are a series of filmstrips designed to teach children to see phrases accurately and read from left to right. The child is helped to correct poor reading habits. Twelve filmstrips and guide from Educational Activities, Inc., Freeport, L. I., N. Y. 11520.

Progressive Visual Perceptual Training Filmstrips Level I by Katherine H. O'Connor is a series of five filmstrips developed to help the student raise his visual perceptual skills. Look alike words and word reversals are presented. The child is asked to see, recall and physically reproduce what he saw. Five filmstrips and manual from Educational Activities, Freeport, L. I., N. Y. 11520.

Sensory Awareness is a series of color-sound filmstrips to enrich sensory perception. They are designed to help children use their visual, auditory and tactile senses more effective in their gathering of information in the world around them. Four filmstrips with records or cassettes from Teaching Resources, 100 Boylston Street, Boston, Mass. 02116.

The Art of Seeing is a series of six color sound filmstrips which introduces the student to the language of visual perception and expression. It stimulates the student to make his own discoveries about painting, sculpture, architecture and other media. Six filmstrips with teacher guide and records or cassettes from Warren Schloat Productions, Pleasantville, N. Y. 10570.

Visual Discrimination Training Filmstrips is a series of filmstrips designed to develop speed and accuracy in recognizing likeness and differences in pictures from letters, numbers, words, phrases, and sentences. Ten filmstrips and manual from Educational Activities, Inc., Freeport, L. I., N. Y. 11520.

Visual Perception Skills is a series of filmstrips designed to aid in the development of basic visual skills. Visual perception is promoted through activities involving visual memory, visual motor coordination, visual constancy, visual discrimination, visualization, figure ground perception and visual matching. Seven color filmstrips and guide from Educational Activities, Inc., Freeport, L. I., N. Y. 11520.

Records

Creative Movement and Rhythmic Exploration (AR 533) by Hap Palmer. Exciting songs provide action and challenges for the child in creative movement, mimetics, and physical activity. Ways to move, geometric shapes, concepts and sounds are explored.*

Developing Perceptual Motor Needs of Primary Level Children (AR 606-7). This record provides a training program to help pupils establish necessary perceptual-motor skills in agility, balance, combination balance and locomotor agility, turning, and complex locomotor agility.*

Discovery through Movement Exploration (AR 534) by Layne C. Hackett. Children are challenged to seek motor solutions to problems in space awareness classroom related activities, ball and rope handling.*

Dynamic Balancing Activities (AR 657) This album is useful for training the child in both static and moving balance activities. These activities combined with various tasks should heighten the child's awareness of his body image.*

Dynamic Balancing Activities: Balance Beam Activities (AR 658). The activities in this album correlate balance and body image activities. The activities range from simple walking in various positions on the beam to more complex balance activities.*

Homemade Band (AR 545) by Hap Palmer. Directions are provided for making home instruments so the child can perform as a member of a band. The suggested activities should help the child in the development of body awareness, gross and fine motor coordination, auditory discrimination, rhythm and freedom of movement.*

Getting To Know Myself (AR 543) by Hap Palmer. This "introduction to learning" covers such areas as awareness of body image and the body's position in space; identification of body places; objects in relation to body planes, body part identification; movements of body, laterality of body, feelings and moods.*

---

*The records may be ordered from Educational Activities, Inc., Freeport, L. I., N. Y. 11520.

Learning Basic Skills Through Music, Volume I (AR 514) by Hap Palmer. Numbers, colors, the alphabet, and body awareness are presented in a happy rhythmic teaching program which is appropriate for pre-school slow learners, and early primary children. The record is also available in Spanish.*

Learning Basic Skills Through Music: Vocabulary (AR 521) by Hap Palmer. Through active participation, the child learns safety vocabulary, kinds of foods, parts of the body, and forms of transportation.*

Learning Basic Skills Through Music, Volume II (AR 522) by Hap Palmer. Games, songs teaching eleven colors, numbers to twenty, subtraction and telling time are included. There are also two reading-readiness game songs. This record is also available in Spanish.*

Math Readiness: Vocabulary and Concepts (AR 540) by Hap Palmer. Concepts such as big, little, long, short, shorter, same, like, different, before, after, in between, greater, and less are explored to help the child in math readiness.*

Music for Movement Exploration (KEA 5090) by Karol Lee. Unique musical effects bring out the original in each child.*

Relaxation—Impulse Control Through Relaxation (AR 655). This record introduces muscle activities to decrease levels of stimulation and increase muscular control. Children are helped to relax, to go slow and to think.*

Simple Agility Movements for Impulse Control (AR 656). This album provides instructions for relaxation training as well as activities to aid children in controlling tension in specific parts of their body rather than permitting a spillover of tensions in all body parts when movement in only one part is desired.*

Sensorimotor Training in the Classroom (AR 532) by Linda Williams and Donna Wemple. Songs, cheers, folk music, chants, popular music and poems are used with selected perceptual activities to develop body image, laterality, space directionality, basic movement, physical fitness, ocular training and auditory discrimination.*

The Development of Body Awareness and Position in Space (AR 605). This record provides a researched training program to aid the student in awareness of his body and position in space.*

To Move Is To Be (KEA 8060) by Jo Ann Scher. Some twenty rock to classical musical selections guide the child into doing his own version of moving, bending, twisting, stretching, hopping, walking, and running.*

---

*The records may be ordered from Educational Activities, Inc., Freeport, L.I., N.Y. 11520.

Teaching Aids

I. These materials from TEACHING RESOURCES CORPORATION* may be used to develop basic skills of visual and tactile discrimination, classification and sorting, order and sequence, position and orientation, comparison and association.

The recognition of shape, form and texture; the ability to determine sameness or difference by comparing properties, orientation, or quantity to classify or group together things that are alike; and the ability to relate body position, both to self and other objects are among the very basic skills in which a child must develop proficiency in order to cope with everyday tasks and function academically.

Alike/Unalike, (81-120). This set of eight books is designed to develop skills discrimination. Concepts of sameness and difference along with the child's ability to recognize and classify a variety of shapes.

Base Materials Resource List, (50-190). A resource box which offers an almost endless number of individualized or group activities to develop and reinforce perceptual skills with early learners. Many areas of perceptual skill training including color and shape recognition; classification; order and sequencing, orientation and position in space; concepts for sets; size and number and quality are possible with this wealth of materials and ideas.

Body Position Cards, (16-510). This motor training program provides a variety of movement experiences to develop basic motor skills and to build the child's sense of command over his own body. The teacher's guide suggests a variety of activities to help develop body awareness, laterality, directionality, spatial judgement, ability to follow directions, balance, agility and flexibility of movement.

Geometric Shapes, (10-130). Two groups of 66 cards teach names of colors, recognition of basic shapes, concepts of spatial orientation, position, sequence, order and quantity and abstract associations from the known to the unknown.

Letter Recognition, (81-130). This series of eight strip books applies visual discrimination to the recognition of letters of the alphabet. Letters appear in varying positions, and most commonly confused or reversed letters are shown.

Percepto Mats, (50-199). These mats help the student make the transition from 3-dimensional level of gross-motor activity to the 2-dimensional level of abstract tasks. Four mats printed with large geometric shapes and the teaching guide offer activities to develop skills of gross-motor coordination, as well as shape recognition, visual figure ground discrimination, auditory memory and the ability to follow directions.

Spatio Match, (81-230). Three decks of cards which help to develop the students' ability to perceive sequence and directional orientation of abstract symbols. This aids in later ability to distinguish between letters which are similar in configuration and to perceive the sequence of letters in words.

These materials may be ordered from:

*Teaching Resources Corporation
100 Boylston Street
Boston, Mass. 02116

II.   Childcraft offers a variety of materials to aid the child with letters, sounds and words. These materials could also be used with games in part III of text.

Tactile Letter Blocks—These large numbers and letters provide a kinesthetic experience which helps the child comprehend letter concepts. (Childcraft)

Touch Teaching Aids—These alphabet cards employ the tactile-kinesthetic method of instruction. The raised surface provides additional sensory experience which will speed recognition of letters for some children. (Childcraft)

Wonder Spelling Kit—This set contains 120 lower case and 26 capital letters in a natural finish plywood. (These could be used for many of the reading, spelling, and writing games in Chapter II, Part III.) (Childcraft)

In addition to the above, Childcraft offers a variety of materials appropriate for children to use in studying shape, color, size, likenesses and differences, space, patterns, and position. A catalog may be requested from Childcraft.

These materials may be ordered from:

Childcraft
Education Corporation
964 Third Ave.
New York, N.Y. 10022

III. Educational Activities, Inc. offers teaching materials to help the teacher with perceptual-motor activities.

Sound, Words, and Actions—This card file contains movement games to help build skills in language arts. The games fulfill the child's inherent need to move as well as helping him to read and deal with words and letter symbols. (Educational Activities, Inc.)

A catalog of materials may be requested from:

Educational Activities, Inc.
Freeport,
L.I., N.Y. 11520

IV. Fairbanks-Robinson Program 11 Level 1: Perceptual-Motor Development by Jean S. Fairbanks and Janet I. Robinson presents tasks which develop perceptual-motor abilities which are considered prerequisite to academic functioning. Activities include tracing, coloring, matching, selecting, and cutting, and activities to develop shape recognition, spatial orientation, constancy of form and size, figure ground discrimination and spatial relationships. Teaching Resources, 100 Boylston St., Boston, Mass. 02116.

Fairbanks-Robinson Program 1 Level 2: Perceptual-Motor Development by Jean S. Fairbanks and Jan I. Robinson is a perceptual-motor program which works with visual manipulation and coordinative experiences. Activities are provided which stress left-to-right movement, top-to-bottom progression, eye-hand coordination, line and form reproduction, ordering of forms by size, part-whole organization, design copying and spatial relationships. Teaching Resources, 100 Boylston St., Boston, Mass. 02116.

Move-Grow-Learn by Marianne Frostig is a movement education program to enhance the development of young children by improving physical, creative, and perceptual development. This program, designed for preschool and primary children promotes good health, a sense of well being and the development of sensory motor skills. It is also designed to develop self-awareness, awareness of time and space, and the ability to communicate, to interact with others, to perceive self in relation to environment, to solve problems and to learn. Follett Publishing Company, Box 5705, Chicago, Ill. 60680.

Pathway School Program 1: Eye-Hand Coordination Exercises by G.N. Getman assists children in acquiring skills of discrimination and dexterity needed for success in classroom performance. The child is helped in using his hands and eyes and in directional control for accuracy. The program may be used with kindergarten and primary children to help prepare them in readiness for reading and writing. Teaching Resources, 100 Boylston St., Boston, Mass. 02116.

Homemade Equipment

Mats —Using a piece of 3' x 5' styrofoam 3'' thick, cover it with a heavy piece of material (canvas, sail cloth) and sew it in place.

Jump Ropes — A hank of sash cord or clothes line works nicely. The length of the rope should be approximately equal to the height of the child. The ends can be tied or taped to prevent unraveling.

Bean Bags — Navy beans sewn in canvas or other suitable study material is fine. Cut the material in 5'' x 5'' squares.

Bean bags of different shapes is also a good idea.

Balance Beam — Make them about 8' in length using 2'' x 4''. If you construct this type of base, the beam can be either 2'' or 4'' in width when using.

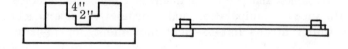

Wands — Cut broom or mop handles into three to four feet sections.

Balance Board — Cut a piece of 3/4'' plywood into a 15'' square. Attach a small 2'' x 2'' block of wood in the middle of the square.

Side Bottom

Painted patterns on available floor surface —

Hula Hoops — Black plastic plumbing tubing and plastic dowels are joined to form any size circle you desire. A standard size hoop is 8' in circumference and 1/2'' thick. A 1 x 1/2'' dowel is used to join the ends.

Footprints — Cut carpet squares work well.

Carpet Square